Choice, Desire and the Will of God: What More Do You Want?

D0931952

Choice, Desire and the Will of God: What More Do You Want?

David Runcorn

Hendrickson Publishers, Inc.
P.O. Box 3473
Peabody, MA 01961-3473

ISBN 1-56563-892-1

First published in Great Britain in 2003 by
Society for Promoting Christian Knowledge
Holy Trinity Church
Marylebone Road
London NW1 4DU

Typeset by Pioneer Associates, Perthshire
Printed in Great Britain by
MPG Books, Bodmin, Cornwall

Hendrickson Publishers' edition reprinted by arrangement with
the Society for Promoting Christian Knowledge.

Hendrickson Edition First Printing — 2003

I saw that those simple things might be true.
You can believe in something without
compromising the burden of your own existence.
Sebastian Faulks, *Birdsong*

You must go and find out.
You must go and discover whether there is anything
in that world for you.
Promise me that you will go.
Andrew Harvey, *A Journey in Ladakh*

Contents

Acknowledgements

This book has been a long time in the planning but it needed a period of sabbatical leave to finally get it started. Trinity College has been a wonderfully stimulating place for testing ideas. I am very grateful to my colleagues and successive student communities for their encouragement, interest – and loving tolerance, in the midst of pressured college life, of my obsessive preoccupations.

I owe special thanks to Simon Awcock, John Bimson, Roger Hurding, my brother Nigel Runcorn and Jane Williams, who all read and offered very helpful comments on sections of the book. My dear late friend Brother Ramon blessed its earliest stages with typical enthusiasm. Sr Christine Head and the community at Llannerchwen, near Brecon, were very significant at an important stage of writing. 'Interlude' is dedicated to them. Finally, I am honoured and very grateful to Archbishop Rowan Williams for writing the Foreword to the book.

Resuming friendship and partnership with Simon Kingston at SPCK has been one of the real pleasures of this project.

Writing is a lonely task and not just for the author. My sons Joshua and Simeon have deserved more energy and attention than I have had to give. I owe them a lot of football and I intend to make it up. This book is gladly dedicated to them.

My thanks above all to my wife, Jackie. In her, choice, desire and the will of God find joyful fulfilment. I am very grateful. It was a long labour and she was a wonderful midwife.

Foreword

I have read few books in recent years that have struck me so much with their emotional honesty. Don't put it down straight away: I don't mean by emotional honesty a chat-show exhibitionism that bores and embarrasses, but a careful statement of the exciting and disturbing and sometimes unstable frontier between doctrine and experience. David Runcorn assumes that what God does relates to us as potential adults, whose sense of themselves is often turbulent and complicated; that God deals with our real desires, not our reluctantly volunteered religious preferences; that nothing will save us from the need for responsibility and discernment.

Here then is a very contemporary account of discipleship that is also not in the least fashionable. It takes seriously the worrying idea that our contemporary styles of life are designed not so much to gratify us as to prevent our *real* desires being met – that we can't cope with working at what we really, as humans, want. David's searching reading in Chapter 9 of the parable of the Prodigal Son brings this powerfully into focus, reminding us that power, even freedom as we commonly understand it, can be a way of avoiding passion. And learning who we are and could be is not a task we can carry through without becoming acquainted with passion: ours and God's.

One of the alarming things about modernity as most of us experience it is that we have very very few recognised tactics in our culture for examining, deepening and educating desire; we are happier to stay at the surface level of itches and scratches, hasty and superficial versions of what we think we want that keep us at a distance from the wanting that hurts and tells us we are by nature needy. We waste untold energies in our Christian life sometimes in argument about issues that divide us, without ever giving a hint that Christian faith might offer resources for such an examination and education. We have heard it said that *metanoia*, the Greek word for 'repentance' in the New Testament, really means 'change of mind' – and we have interpreted this as if it meant changing the contents of our ideas box rather than changing the very way we understand and live out our desire. It would not be wrong to say that this is a book about conversion, true conversion, a change of the habits of the self and its thoughts and images; and we badly need such books, since we are all capable of living as Christians, even 'converted' Christians, with some very unconverted habits of the heart.

This is a wise, entertaining, poignant work, a joy and a challenge to read. May it help all its readers towards its author's honesty and trustfulness.

Rowan Williams

The spaciousness of God

> It is
> meant to
> be what
> it is —
> a free for
> all . . .

WHAT MORE do you want?

I don't mean this book in your hand.
We are creatures of desire.
We want things, deeply and passionately.
We are never more revealed than in our
    longings.
So the deepest mystery of who we are lies
buried in this question.
We do not approach it lightly.

At first glance this looks an ideal world and time for creatures of desire. The opportunities have never been greater. The freedom to have what we want and to be who we wish is one of the defining ideals of western society. To serve that freedom our political and commercial life is ordered around the endless proliferation and stimulation of personal choice. We know ourselves by choice. Western dominance of world markets ensures we have opportunities to pursue this in a way of life undreamed of by previous generations.

So why aren't we happier? Repeated social surveys reveal a culture ill at ease with itself. This adventure is proving very elusive. There is very little freedom about the way we live and the evidence is we are not fooled. The most commonly reported concerns of people seeking counselling is a general sense of exhaustion and powerlessness. We find ourselves overwhelmed by a complex mixture of commitments and requirements that we have little memory of ever agreeing to.

Something missing

We are restless. We need somewhere to ask questions. It may not be that anything has gone particularly wrong for us – at least on the surface. But we live with the quiet despair of knowing, deep down, that in some utterly fundamental way we are missing the point. Like the man who can no longer ignore a dull ache of dissatisfaction that nothing fills. He has reached mid-life, with achievements that would appear enviably fulfilling to anyone looking on. But he has come to a point of admitting he does not know himself. Where is he to begin? Or the woman who is starting to question the hectic busyness of her lifestyle. It has been exciting. She is popular and living life to the full. But 'what would happen if I stopped? Would there be anything? I feel I have no home. Something inside me is just living out of an emotional suitcase – and I fear that even that is empty.'

One of the wisest books in recent years is an extended reflection on the experience of 'overwhelming' that characterises so much of our living today.[1]

Opting in

Freedom is the central gift in the Christian faith. It is the freedom to enter into a completely new relationship with God. This in turn liberates our relationship with each other and our world. One of the most evocative ways the Bible expresses this new life is in terms of spaciousness. 'He brought me out into a broad place, he delivered me because he delighted in me' (Psalm 18.19).

It was in this spirit that some of the first Christians called themselves 'deserters for God'. But they were not opting out of the world into some narrow religious ghetto. Rather they found a joyful spaciousness to live in the world without being confined, manipulated and squeezed into its mould. Christian freedom is radical and disturbing and that is why, throughout history, it has attracted persecution. People still die for it.

Yet this freedom too is elusive. If it were so self-evidently what we wanted we would have entered it long ago. 'Spaciousness' is not the word many would choose to describe their experience of faith. Religion is better known for narrowing and denying life than for liberating it. Richard Holloway once remarked, 'So much religion is an attempt to tame the madness of God.' A great deal of the New Testament is written for communities that were struggling to stay true to the freedom that is their vocation.

Faithful freedom

'Christ has set us free to live a free life,' St Paul urges. 'So take your stand! Never again let anyone put a harness of slavery on you' (Galatians 5.1, *The Message*). He goes on to challenge the Church about the temptation to turn their faith into a system of rules and regulations. Christian faith is about living as free people.

How interesting that even Christians close to the living source of the faith should be behaving in this way. Paul likens them to slaves who have been given their freedom but who keep trying to put their chains back on.

I once had to prepare a sermon on this passage and was struggling with how to apply Paul's words to the Church today, and to my own faith. Was I allowing, in some way, the 'harness of slavery' to be refitted onto my life? Where was I giving away my Christian freedom for the more familiar security of captivity? The answer, when it came, was completely unexpected. With a firm conviction I came to recognise that I had been giving my freedom away to *God*.

This was nothing to do with faith. For me 'the will of God' had become a way of avoiding making my own decisions. When it suited me, my faith regressed into a kind of wilful slavery – hiding behind God from the life that was mine to live. There was no need to wrestle with the dilemmas and consequences of actions. This had the added advantage of looking impressively spiritual!

The experience led me first of all to examine my relationship with myself. This was something I had learned that Christians *didn't* do. Commitment to Jesus was about turning away from ourselves. It was about self-denial. But how can we give ourselves away, if we have yet to meet ourselves? I knew my need to build a relationship with my own choices, desires and longings. I needed to grow up. I found a good counsellor.

More important still, it led me to question and deepen my understanding of God, of his will and of my life within it. I revisited my Bible and sought to deepen my praying. Many of the themes explored in this book began to emerge during this period of my life.

Struggling with guidance

Another influence on this book has been the experience of working with men and women training for Christian ministry and leadership. This has meant sharing their lives at a particularly significant time of personal formation. The task requires careful discerning of choice and desires, and seeking the Spirit of God in it all is central to the task.

It is probably at the times when we face important life choices that the shape of our faith is most sharply revealed. The 'problem of guidance' is one of the abiding mysteries of the Christian life. It can leave normally mature and well-balanced people in knots of anxious uncertainty.

I have always found books on guidance very frustrating. Even the best of them struggle to avoid becoming 'how to' books. The whole concern is too easily narrowed to the issue of 'what God wants' in a particular situation. Our technological mindset, with its problem/solution approach to life, encourages this tendency. But our whole lived experience is involved at such times. The exhilarating and baffling mystery of knowing our lives caught up in the love and purposes of God cannot be reduced to spiritual techniques. Method is no substitute for mystery. It was this attitude that Thomas Merton was sending up when he took a photograph that showed an enormous industrial hook on the end of a thick chain hanging down against a blank sky. He called it 'The only known photo of God'.

Living out of our depth

What if this whole enterprise is much wider, wilder and more adventurous than we have begun to imagine? A therapist once commented on a client who had withdrawn from counselling. 'He wanted me to make him into a better choice-maker. I wanted to help him become a better risk-taker.' This book is written out of a suspicion that God often feels the same about us.

> *When you look at us, at me, what pains you most?*
> The unlived life. The prison of smallness. And more terrible evils that spring from the shrinking of the heart.[2]

Our vocation is to imagine the world as God does. It is a world of endless choice and possibility. To be made alive in

Christ is to be called into the same adventurous spirit of life which brought this world to birth. Such a vocation involves the whole of our humanity. We must learn to listen to our own depths. The problem with our age is not that we pay too much attention to our wants and passions. We do not take our longings seriously enough. We must befriend our desires.[3] We must learn to live in our choices. If this calls us to a life of responsibility it is also an invitation to extraordinary freedom. But above all else this path will call us to a constant renewing of our vision of God. This is a vocation to contemplation, wonder and mystery. Nothing could be more glorious or more demanding.

To explore these themes, this book is offered more as a conversation than a systematic study. It is a search for the broad place of God's delight, towards the joyful unfolding of all unlived life in the free gift of divine love.

CHAPTER 1

As it is in heaven

Incarnation, Trinity and the dancing secret

> The incarnation is God's most daring, reckless invitation.

GOD'S DESIRE is revealed in our bodies.
Pardon?
'God's desire is revealed in our bodies.' It's a quote. I like it.
That's going a bit far, isn't it?
Why?
Well, for one thing, it is so improbable. I mean, you try standing in front of a full-length mirror first thing in the morning and saying that.
  I agree it is a mystery. Being loved always is. But if someone declares their desire for us it is not for us to tell them they are wrong. That is their gift to give. So what do you think the incarnation is all about, then?
  That's easy. God made the world good. It has gone badly wrong. God loves it so much he sent his Son, Jesus, to save us from our sins and to bring us back to him.
  OK. I believe that too. But are you saying we would have never met Jesus if things had not gone wrong? I mean, for the Creator to become a creature is such an amazing thing to do. Did he only come as a human being to put things right here and then leave again? Is the incarnation like God calling himself out as an earthly repairman?

A body like ours

What the incarnation tells us before anything else is that God is caught up in an unlikely, undying love affair with our humanity. To take flesh has been his hidden desire since before time began.

The secret is now out. Rubem Alves puts it even more daringly: 'What the doctrine of the incarnation whispers to us is that God, from all eternity, wants a body like ours.'[1]

This takes a bit of thinking out. It will certainly change how we talk about the Christian faith. We know that Jesus came into the world because of God's love, but we still actually put the emphasis in the story firmly elsewhere. It is usually told in terms of a divine rescue mission. Jesus comes to be our Saviour; he comes into this sinful world to sort things out; he comes because we are in need; through the cross he restores us to fellowship with God our Father.

All of which is wonderfully true. The cross is absolutely central to Christian faith and to salvation. But the story does not begin there. If that is our whole understanding of the incarnation, we are putting the needs of our sinful humanity in the centre instead of God. The coming of Jesus belongs to a much bigger, more mysterious and more glorious vision.

The Bible teaches that the love that Jesus uniquely expressed in the human form is the same love the world has known from the beginning. In the overture that begins John's Gospel Jesus is introduced as none other than the eternal 'Word' who was there in the beginning, the creative source of all life. 'All things came into being through him, and without him not one thing came into being' (John 1.3). 'In him all things in heaven and earth were created, things visible and invisible – all things have been created through him and for him . . . and in him all things hold together' (Colossians 1.15–17). This is the one who 'sustains all things by his powerful word' (Hebrews 1.3).

All creation is the work of Christ. The incarnation is the fulfilling of God's original plan of and for creation. It is not a solution to a problem dreamed up in God's merciful imagination ('I know, I'll try this'). It is much more than God taking our humanity. In the end it is about the taking of our humanity in God.

At the beginning of his letter to the church in Ephesus, St Paul sums up the whole Christian story as a long-kept secret that God wants to let everyone in on. In a passage littered with words like 'love', 'blessing', 'lavished', 'glorious grace', 'hope', he writes: 'God has allowed us to know the secret of his plan and it is this: he purposes in his sovereign will that all human history shall be consummated in Christ, that everything that exists in heaven or earth shall find its perfection and fulfilment in him' (Ephesians 1.9, J. B. Phillips).

The first sign

One of the Gospels chooses to launch the earthly ministry of Jesus with an unexpected account of a village wedding that Jesus attended with his family (John 2.1–11). The story is well known. The wine runs out at the reception. The celebration is in danger of drying up almost before it has started. Behind the scenes, Jesus takes action and the result is startling. He turns more than 330 litres of water into what the master of ceremonies describes as the best wine he has ever drunk. This after the guests had already drunk their way through the original supply! This is more than generous. It is irresponsible – even mischievous. Isn't there a moral issue here? (What excuses did the guests offer when they were late into work the next day – 'God gave me a hangover'?) John calls this miracle the 'first sign' of Jesus. Not simply first among many – but the '*Arch*sign'. This is *the* sign that is the key to interpreting all the signs that follow. This sign 'revealed his glory and his disciples believed in him'.

What is it a sign of? It is a sign that a wildly generous, intoxicating, joyful love is now revealed in the world. A love that never stops at what is strictly *necessary*. This love will transform beyond all that is needed or the occasion requires. To contemplate the glory of God revealed at the launch of Jesus' earthly ministry this is what we must picture: a small village wedding party surely in an advanced state of joyful, helpless inebriation, as yet oblivious to the true source of their blessing!

What is it a sign of? God's love among us. The world is a wedding.

Down to earth

'If you want to contemplate God at this time of year', a friend said, one Christmas, 'you must picture a foetus in its mother's womb, bumping along in the dark on the back of a donkey.' It is not easy to imagine God eternally desiring to make his home in our mortal flesh. 'These sweaty hormone-driven bodies make an unlikely tabernacle for the divine.'[2] Something in this message moves me to my depths. But I am ambivalent too. The incarnation means that our searching for God must also involve a searching for ourselves in all our muddled, worldly humanity. God wills that we cannot know heaven without also knowing earth.

Beyond all expectation this messy, physical, human existence is intimately caught up into the mystery of God's desiring. He takes flesh. And ours is involved too. We cannot know God without also knowing our own fleshly humanity. The heart of our life's pilgrimage is to come to a place where we love ourselves and our earthly existence the way God loves us. This is what it means to follow Jesus.

This will often involve seeking God in and through what we would rather avoid. It is always tempting to go looking for a different kind of salvation. I never quite lose the hope that 'rescue' means being taken somewhere else. I really want a transformation like those in the perennially popular television programmes where we watch someone's very ordinary front lounge or rambling garden being completely gutted and turned into something totally new and fantastically creative – usually while they are away and without their knowledge. It is finished just seconds before the unsuspecting person returns home. Surprise!

Ah, if only life were like that – you come home one day and find that the wearying unresponsive muddle has vanished and a designer life is just waiting for you to open your eyes.

The human face of God

> Your kingdom come,
> your will be done,
> on earth as it is in heaven

The words are so familiar. But what exactly are we asking for? It may seem self-evident that life would be better down here if God were in charge the way we imagine he is in heaven. But if this prayer were to be answered, what do we imagine life here would be like?

The incarnation brings us to a new meeting with ourselves in our earthly humanity. It also brings us to a new vision of God. The incarnation makes God visible. Jesus states this explicitly: 'Whoever has seen me has seen the Father' (John 14.9). Other New Testament teachers are equally emphatic: 'He is the image [literally the 'icon', 'exact likeness'] of the invisible God' (Colossians 1.15). Christ is 'the reflection of God's glory, the exact imprint of God's very being' (Hebrews 1.3). 'In him all the fullness of God was pleased to dwell' (Colossians 1.19).

Not surprisingly this is another point at which this extraordinary story gets distorted. Not only is the coming of Jesus reduced to a rescue mission, but in the struggle to express the costliness of his gift, we can easily give the impression that his coming, suffering and dying was somehow an extra-special effort on God's part – after trying everything else.

I heard an example of this in a challenging sermon on the subject of Christian service. The preacher told the story of the final meal Jesus shared with his disciples on the night before he died. Jesus shocked everyone by suddenly behaving like the household slave and washing everyone else's feet. Trying to underline just how radical it was for the Son of God to behave like this, the preacher described Jesus as 'setting aside his divine status' and performing an 'unGodlike' act.

But clearly Jesus does not think it is unusual for God to behave like that. Jesus does not have to set aside anything Godly to act like a humble servant. He is not acting out of divine character. God's love is like this. Take a closer look. In this serving, humble, suffering, self-giving, cross-bearing gift of Jesus, God is just being himself!

God's antique

The incarnation is an invitation to be united in the life of God, the Holy Trinity. We know that Jesus longed and prayed for this: 'As you, Father, are in me and I am in you, may they also be in us, that the world may believe' (John 17.21).

The doctrine of the Holy Trinity has had an unhappy place in the life of the Church for too long. By the end of my training for ministry I knew that the Holy Trinity was *very important*. But it could only be explained by experts using Greek words and highly philosophical concepts (which for the most part had eluded me). At work, the Trinity was possibly best pictured as a kind of very, *very* efficient committee, managing the creation, rescue and restoration of this fallen world. But its place in the life of the Church was that of a theological antique. It was very old, possibly priceless (though no one was quite sure). So no one would think of getting rid of it, but it was of no practical use.

Yet in recent years there has been an exciting rediscovery of this doctrine and the revelation it offers of the life of God, Father, Son and Holy Spirit. There is a famous passage in the letter to the Philippians that offers a way in. Paul is urging the Church to live and love the way Christ does and he includes some verses that are possibly from a very early Christian hymn. 'Let the same mind be in you that was in Christ Jesus,' writes Paul,

> who, though he was in the form of God
> did not regard equality with God
> as something to be exploited,
> but emptied himself,
> taking the form of a slave,
> being born in human likeness . . .
> he humbled himself (Philippians 2.6–8)

But this popular translation distorts what the verse is saying. 'Though he was in the form of God' suggests that in heaven Jesus would have been within his rights to insist on his status but he chose not to. This again gives the impression that in the incarnation and the cross God is acting contrary to what is normally his way.

A better translation is:

> *Precisely because* he was in the form of God
> he did not consider being equal with God
> grounds for grasping.
> On the contrary, he poured himself out . . .
> by taking the form of a slave,
> being born in human likeness . . .
> he humbled himself.[3]

'*Precisely because*'. For the Son of God to pay any attention to his own status or importance, to claim privileges, or to use his name and influence for his own ends, is quite unthinkable. To be God-like is *not* to be grasping. On the contrary, to be God-like is to empty yourself out in humble love. The life of God is non-possessive, non-competitive, humbly attentive to the interests of the other, united in love and vision. Jesus pours himself out '*precisely because*' he is God from God.

Learning to dance

From earliest days one of the ways Christians have tried to express the life and relationship of the Father, Son and Holy Spirit is as a dance. An early Easter hymn has the words,

O thou leader of the mystic round dance!
O thou leader of the spiritual marriage feast.

Two words are important for understanding what kind of dance this is and what it might be like to join it. Describing a relationship, the word *perichoresis* means a free, mutual exchange. The life of each is continuously fulfilled by the gift of the others in an eternal, non-grasping dance of mutual indwelling. 'They not only encircle each other and weave in and out of each other as in human dancing; in the divine dance, so intimate is the communion that they move in and through each other so that the pattern is all-inclusive'.[4] It is a dance that is only possible because the life of the Holy Trinity is one of pure giving.

This is where the other key word appears – *kenosis*. It is a word used to speak of how Jesus *emptied* himself. But when Jesus emptied himself to enter our world as human being, he was acting and loving out of the dance of the Holy Trinity.

So the incarnation offers us a mysterious and astonishing vision – the Holy Trinity as a dancing community of divine poverty. Each eternally, joyfully, dispossessing themselves; emptying, pouring themselves out to the favour and glory of the other. Nothing claimed, demanded or grasped. They live and know each other in the simple ecstasy of giving.

We are invited to participate in this dance. There are accounts in early Christian writings of churches expressing their prayer through dance. God's desire from before all time has been to draw us into it.

Participation

It is my daily habit to pray before the rest of the family wake up. One morning I heard a knock on the door of the shed that is my hermitage. My son Joshua stood there in the dark, shivering, smiling but searching my face, a little uncertain of his welcome. We cuddled for warmth in the soft candlelight, quietly looking at the icons. One of them is the well-known icon of the Holy Trinity by André Rublev.

The Father, Son and Holy Spirit are sitting on three sides of a table. There is a deep and gentle reverence in their awareness of each other. The Son and the Spirit are inclining their heads towards the Father. The Father is inclining towards the Son and the Spirit. There is a beautiful, silent flow of living attentiveness that could almost be a dancing. Something in their relationship leaves me feeling almost embarrassed after a while. I feel as if I am an intruder into something intimate and very private. But as in all icons the perspective is inverse. That is to say the picture opens out towards the watcher. This is deliberate. The picture draws us in and invites our participation. The table has a space kept on our side. The scene will not be complete until we have taken our place.

Joshua and I began to talk about it. *Do you think they know we are watching them? What do you think they might say to us?*

I suggest: 'Come on, Josh, come on, Daddy, join us, we're waiting for you. We can't really start without you!'

Joshua's face breaks into a broad grin at the thought. Then we are both giggling with pleasure at the imagining of it.

'I'll have sausages, beans and chips,' said Joshua, emphatically.

CHAPTER 2

If God is God
Omnipotence, love and divine freedom

> Omnipotence is a mistake — though it is an easy one to make if you want God to be as powerful as possible.

DEAR GOD,
I don't often sit down and write to you. But there's a difficult question that I want to ask. It's bothered me for a while now and it's this: Do you *really* know everything – absolutely everything? You see, I can't help feeling disappointed if you do. And (forgive me if this sounds disrespectful) I can't help feeling you are missing something if you do.

Take surprises, for example. You can never be surprised. If you know everything, nothing catches you out. But that's an awful thought to me. Have you really never experienced a moment completely unexpected – the delicious thrill of a complete surprise – a gift of love and fun that was kept a secret though we nearly burst! Can't I tell you my favourite joke without you knowing the punchline already and pretending to laugh, like grown-ups do for children? I don't like the thought of that.

And there are three of you, aren't there? Do you know everything about each other – and if so, what is there to talk about? Isn't it boring? Aren't there any secrets – like what you are getting for Christmas? Can you never creep up behind each other for fun and make each other jump and laugh?

Don't you see, this affects me too. It frustrates me that there's bits of me it seems we cannot share. Is 'surprise' a gift you've given me that wasn't yours to give? Sometimes, in a playful mood, I want to creep up quietly behind you and suddenly burst upon you with my loudest joy – and see you jump! See your growing smile, and feel the delight of your encircling arms and hear you whisper, 'me too, me too'.

But I can't if you know already. And it wouldn't be the same if I thought you were just pretending for me. And so I have a fear inside. I'm afraid that if you know everything, you must be rather serious.

Ever yours,
Guess who?

The theological wallpaper of Christendom

The crumbling walls of our once-Christian western civilisation are decorated with some very ancient theological wallpaper. Although it is fading, the original power and beauty of its awesome, majestic theme – the Christian vision of God – can still be felt. For centuries no other wallpaper was even imaginable in the home of Christendom. So complete was its design and so enduring its quality that to change it seemed unthinkable.

One of the things about wallpaper is that we quickly stop noticing it. We relate to the once carefully chosen features of our own homes with the unconsidering familiarity that comes with daily routine unless something draws our attention to them. In the same way, this theological wallpaper has been in place so long that we may not be conscious of its effect on us, our thinking, our praying and the whole 'feel' of the living space that is our life.

So what are the dominant themes and designs that characterise this wallpaper? They start from the simple conviction that if God is God then he must be the absolute sovereign over all things. God is utterly transcendent. In his own being he dwells in eternity, outside time and space. He is everywhere (omnipresent). His power is limitless and he can act and effect whatever he chooses (omnipotent). He is changeless (immutable). He does not suffer or feel pain (impassible). He knows all things – past, present and future (omniscient).

Support can be found in the Bible for this view. Isaiah's vision of God in the temple is one of awesome transcendence (Isaiah 6.1). St Paul teaches 'it is he [God] alone who has immortality and dwells in unapproachable light' (1 Timothy 6.16) and declares 'the immeasurable greatness of his power' (Ephesians 1.19). Through the prophet Isaiah God forthrightly declares, 'I form light and create darkness, I make weal and create woe, I the Lord do all these things' (Isaiah 45.7). Samuel reveals a God who 'will not recant or change his mind. He is not a mortal, that he should change his mind' (1 Samuel 15.29). In the prophecies of Malachi God promises, 'I the Lord do not change' (Malachi 3.6). And does not Psalm 139 affirm God's complete knowledge of us and his preordained will for all of life? 'Even before a word is on my tongue, O Lord, you know it completely', and 'in your book were written all the days that were formed for me, when none of them as yet existed' (vv. 4 and 16).

To this God many in the Church have attached some further definitions: his will ordains all that happens; it is irresistible and infallibly brings about what he chooses; nothing happens that has not been ordained by him; he does not change his mind. God is in control.

By definition

This understanding of God is often taken to be self-evident. This is what God is like *by definition*. We hear this assumption in action whenever a discussion about the power or ability of God is being challenged and someone counters with: 'but surely if God is God then . . .', and one of his absolute attributes of power, knowledge, justice will then be asserted. Such is the power of theological wallpaper. God, by definition, must be *absolutely* God.

There are three main reasons why this way of thinking about God is being increasingly challenged.

First, there is the sheer weight of human pain in a world that has just lived through the most destructive and brutal period in its history. Such experience challenges what we believe about God. If we claim that God rules over this world with absolute power and perfect foreknowledge and that all that happens is a product of his infallible will, then he is the source of all the evil and suffering in the world. Indeed he actually wills it. Is God therefore responsible for war, child abuse, cancer, poverty and starvation? If God is omnipotent and ordains all that happens, then he is surely not good.

Second, what kind of world would such a God bring into being? A world controlled by God's perfect and all-determining will would not be a world in which there is freedom to choose and act. What relationships are possible in an all-programmed creation? The world would be 'a play that God has scripted in eternity that we have no choice but to perform'.

Third, in what sense can this God be said to be *Christian*? Can this be the unseen God revealed uniquely in the life and teaching of Jesus Christ?

Pressed to its logical extreme this description of God is of one who is unfeeling, unresponsive, impersonal, remote and utterly self-contained. It is not easy to know in what sense we can speak of God's love, compassion, mercy, infinite patience and willingness to respond to our prayers. It is hard to imagine this God becoming a human being, and revealing himself through suffering, death and resurrection.

The heart of God

The Bible offers a very different way of understanding the character of God and how he relates to his world.

He creates this world with exhilarating joy – 'that's good!' He is a God who delights in his people (Psalm 149.4). He can be 'deeply moved' (Jeremiah 31.20), or rejoice with noisy singing (Zephaniah 3.17). There are also occasions where God changes his mind or is persuaded to relent from a declared course of action. When God decided to destroy his people after they made a golden calf and worshipped it, Moses intervened, pleading for them, and God 'changed his mind' (Exodus 32.14). Abraham is permitted to enter into prolonged negotiation with God over the fate of Sodom (Genesis 18.20–33).

And what of the story of Jonah? After finally going to Nineveh to declare God's terminal judgment on that city, he is furious when God relents after the city repents (though the terms of the judgment appeared final and non-negotiable). But all this came as no surprise to Jonah. He says he saw this coming all along. 'I knew that you are a gracious God and merciful, slow to anger, and abounding in steadfast love and ready to relent from punishing' (Jonah 4.2).

At a time of spiritual unfaithfulness, God identifies with his prophet Hosea, who is himself going through a very public marriage break-up. God speaks in the same raw terms of heartbreak, pain and deep anger over his rejection and his people's adultery. But he cannot let go of a moving hope for reconciliation and the reawakening of the love that first kindled the relationship. 'Therefore I will now persuade her, and bring her into the wilderness, and speak tenderly to her . . . There she shall respond as in the days of her youth, as at the time when she came out of the land of Egypt' (Hosea 2.14–15).

Finally of course there is the life of Jesus. Through him we meet a God who willingly chooses vulnerability by becoming a human foetus in its mother's womb. He is infinitely responsive to the cries and prayers of his world. He weeps, hurts and groans with angry compassion in the presence of suffering and death. He reveals astonishing mercy and long-suffering, and even forgives those who reject and kill him. This is a God uniquely and universally recognised in the figure hanging from a cross in lonely death for the world he comes to save.

Whose name is love

Imagine that you are being introduced to someone very important. You have been told they will be a life-transforming influence on your life if you only trust them. The information you are given about them includes facts about their extraordinary intelligence, academic achievements and tireless physical strength. They are fabulously wealthy, have worldwide political spheres of influence, have the widest experience of life and possess apparently infallible discernment about people. Is there anything else you would want to ask?

Yes. You have not been told the one thing you most need to know about them – their character. What are they actually like? Are they 'good', 'loving'? You may find their attributes attractive or terrifying, but if you are to trust them you will want to ask what kind of person they are.

Significantly the nearest the Bible gets to a definition of God is 'God is Love' (1 John 4.8). Alongside the refined, technical sophistication of those ancient Greek attributes it sounds almost naive. But those three words change everything. What if God's love and not his absolute power shapes the way he relates to his world?

In the midst of suffering – and especially since the Holocaust – these three words have offered many people a new and more helpful way in to contemplating the mystery of God's presence and action in the world. Approaching God from his love rather than his power will reshape our understanding of him in two significant ways.

The limits of love

If God is love, is he omnipotent? A God of love cannot do just as he chooses. He is constrained by his nature: he is constrained by his love. Real love always gives space and freedom to the beloved. It involves willing self-limiting, self-denial for the sake of the other, so that they may be free to grow and to choose to love also. For God to create us and this world must involve an act of self-limiting. As soon as love is imposed or demanded it ceases to be love. So God can be present in our lives only because he also, by loving choice, withdraws in some way.

The same point was illustrated by two scientists in a television documentary discussing research into artificial intelligence. One said, 'If you want the agent to be free – to be autonomous – and not just a computer program you have written for it – then you have to let it go, let it explore for itself and learn for itself.' The other agreed and then suggested this might be how God creates a world of real freedom and choice. 'It's only when the creator has let go of the system that the system can count as having free will. God couldn't have programmed us in detail. He had to use evolution because only that puts enough distance between God's intention and my intention for my acts to turn out to be free.'

So God's love may limit his absolute power to act and change the world. But it releases new hope of where he may be found within it. God is with us. That is the nature of love. It seeks communion. God's love will be found in the midst of created life, intimately involved, sharing its suffering and struggles. The cross is a visible testimony to this. So although the God of love does not remove suffering from the world, we may meet him in the struggles at the heart of it.[1]

God's own freedom

Trying to define God is a dangerous activity. It should carry a health warning with it. Nor can the discussion be resolved by exchanging a God who is omnipotent (but not good) with a God who is suffering love (but not all-powerful). The hardest thing is to allow God his own freedom. The greatest limitation in all this debate is that we only know how to speak of God in relation to our own world, our needs and longings. It is very hard to let God be God. R. S. Thomas once wrote a moving poem about this, after seeing a rare white tiger at Bristol Zoo. He was overwhelmed by the sheer beauty, grace and potency of that creature. He also felt the contradiction and pain of its captivity, as it paced restlessly up and down in the confinement of a tiny cage. He asks if this isn't how God must feel, within the confines of all our attempts to define and control him.[2]

This was the heart of the problem during the period of Israel's greatest crisis, one that culminated in the destruction of Jerusalem and the long exile of God's people. It was a time of fragmentation, disintegration and chaos. But deeper than the military crisis they were facing was the crisis of theology and faith. The final tragedy of that time lay in the inability of God's people to relate to God in anything other than utilitarian terms. God was *their* God and therefore *must* guard them, bless them, be there for them. Their deepest peril lay not in the imminent threat of invading armies so much as in the departure of God. But as the crisis intensifies, the sense of distance between God and his people grows. The relationship is breaking down and communication is becoming apparently impossible.

There are disturbing parallels with the assumptions that drive western society today. In consumer culture everything is an object. Everything is defined by its usefulness and what it can do for *me*. The Church all too easily succumbs too. Its buildings and worship are now designed for maximum relevance and accessibility to those around. We know what we want to say to each other but are in danger of losing any sense of God's otherness – his glorious and awesome transcendence. God is reduced to a useful commodity.

What did God do in the crisis facing Israel? He refused to be useful. He would not be defined in terms of his people's need of him. As the terrible political and military storm clouds raged over Israel, God left. In that most terrible vision in the Bible, Ezekiel watched as the glory of God departed from Jerusalem (Ezekiel 10).

When a relationship becomes trapped in the (spoken or unspoken) requirement that it meets our needs, rather than that it offers love, it will be marked by unhealthy dependency. It will cease to give life and may become destructive. There may come a point where only one course of action is possible for the future of the relationship and those within it. There has to be a break. Only a radical separation opens the possibility of making something new out of the wreckage.

To think that God may walk out on his world is a terrifying scenario. But the story does not end there. We discover quite unexpectedly that God's own freedom to walk out is precisely where our hope lies. In the first place, his freedom does not make God indifferent as we might expect. To be *un*committed is a human definition of freedom and the social consequence of that belief is all around us. But even where covenants and promises lie broken, God's own free nature presses him to act. So hope that life might find new beginning out of crisis and chaos depends on God *not* having a commitment to his people or to his world. He is free and unbound by the things that bind us. So he is free to choose to bring something new to life out of the ruins of the old.[3]

Letting go of God

Some years ago, in deep personal crisis and close to a breakdown, I spent two months alone in an alpine cabin. I wanted to spend time with God. To my dismay he did not show up. The silence was empty. The familiar comforts of faith and assurance also went missing. I found it both frightening and inexplicable. I wept, shouted and hammered on the walls of the cabin demanding his presence. This was a crisis of faith. How could he not be there for me? How can I believe any more? Who was God anyway? He seemed supremely unimpressed. But no one can sustain a tantrum indefinitely – least of all with an absent God! As I slumped again into sullen silence I was confronted with the nature of my demands. To my cry, 'Who are you?', the silence echoed 'Who are *you*?'

The assumption that God can be summoned for our own fulfilment and security runs deep (though of course we never express it so crudely). We even think God's promises bind him to our needs. We know our consumer rights. There are times when God's absence may be his toughest but most saving gift. For God is free – he cannot be commanded. And in that freedom is our hope. He is not under contract. His love comes as a gift.

Up there in that alpine cabin one morning, there came a tearful and frightening moment. Kneeling on the wooden floor, I told God I would no longer treat him as if I owned him. I confessed the possessiveness and self-absorption that I called 'love for God'. I confessed my attempts to control and dominate. I repented of my inability to love him for himself rather than for what I needed. I let him go. Something died that day – and something was born. The lesson, though, is never finally learned.

> O how I fear thee, living God
>   With deepest, tend'rest fears,
> And worship thee with trembling hope
>   And penitential tears![4]

CHAPTER 3

'Let there be . . .'
Invitation, imagination and the work of creation

> . . . more the appearance of an improvisation than the performance of a predetermined script.

GOD IS USELESS.
I mean he serves no purpose.
He does not need a reason to exist.
Being God is not a job. No one
  appointed him.
He is complete in himself.
He just is.

And that means creation is useless too. God did not need to create the world. He was not lonely or lacking in any way. He does not need our love or worship. So we are not here to make a point. We are not a divinely manufactured product. This world exists simply because God takes pleasure in it. It is free gift sustained in divine delight – a work of boundless imagination.

Evidence for this is everywhere. For one thing there is too much in this world that is simply unnecessary. Creation is wildly extravagant but none of it is just for show. You never reach the edge of the plastering or see where the paint stops when God is at work. This inexhaustible, mind-blowing creativity pours out far beyond all sight and knowledge.

Beginning now

'In the beginning, God created the heavens and the earth' – one of the most famous first lines in world literature. It is usually understood to mean that right at the beginning of time God made (past tense, action completed) the world. But many Bibles have a footnote at the bottom of the page suggesting another way of translating that line: 'In the beginning when God *began creating* the heavens and the earth'. The change of tense changes the mood immediately. There is suddenly a sense of movement. What was once begun still continues. Creation is still in process. It is not yet finished or complete.

This alternative translation is met with suspicion in some Christian circles. I once used a liturgy that included a small change to a traditional response:

Our help is in the name of the Lord
Who made the heavens and the earth.

The second line was adapted in the spirit of the alternative creation reading:

Who is making the heavens and the earth.

The wording provoked strong discussion afterwards. Some people were very anxious that the line was 'New Age'.

When I led a Quiet Day on one occasion I included those lines in a collection of prayers for use during the day. The organisers offered to print and distribute them to everyone. When I came to use the prayers later that day, I found that those two lines, without any discussion or consultation, had been omitted.

But though the Bible is quite clear that this world has a beginning, in God's creating act at the dawn of what we call time, it never speaks of that creation as something finally complete, as though all growing, developing and maturing has been completed too. Psalm 104 celebrates creation as a continuing work. In the midst of a joyful survey of the whole variety of what God has created we read:

When you send forth your spirit they are created
and you (ever) renew the face of the earth. (v. 30)

Most English translations translate the second line 'you renew the face of the earth' and miss the power of that continuous tense. Creation continues to be called into life, renewed and sustained as it was in the beginning.

Play making

At each stage of the creation story in Genesis God pauses, surveys what he has brought into being and declares it 'good'. The word doesn't mean morally good (as opposed to bad or evil). Nor does it refer to technical excellence (i.e. a job well done). The word expresses sheer pleasure – something utterly lovely, beautiful and exhilarating to behold. Creation knows itself in God's desire and pure delight. This sense of infectious joy and celebration is found in a wonderful passage in Proverbs where 'Wisdom' tells of the mutual joy of creation in the presence of God:

I was beside the master craftsman,
Delighting him day after day
Ever at play in his presence,
at play everywhere on his earth,
delighting to be with the human race.[1]

It has been repeatedly vandalised, trashed and horribly misused, but this world still bears all the signs of having been created to be a playground.

Telling the story

Stories are never accidents. By the time they have reached us they have usually lived many lives, travelled long distances and been shared many times. They are born out of people's desires and they awaken our own. They are ways by which we search out what life means and seek our place within the mystery of it.

There are two creation stories at the beginning of the Bible. Like all stories they would have evolved in the telling, but they seem to have found their distinctive Bible voice at quite contrasting times in the history of God's people. They are both pastoral stories, told to minister to very different contexts of human choice, desiring and longing.

The first story (Genesis 1.1—2.3) is thought to date from the sixth century BC in Babylon.[2] That was where God's people had ended up in exile after Jerusalem, their holy city, had been destroyed and their country overrun and ruined. Babylon was the superpower who had conquered them. This experience was more than just a social and military disaster – though that would have been bad enough. It was a total theological annihilation.

Yahweh, their God, had apparently been crushed by Marduk and the gods of the Babylonians. The very foundation of their lives had been shattered. The familiar words of faith and worship had lost their meaning. Like immigrants far from their homeland, they had to start learning a new language.

> By the rivers of Babylon —
>   there we sat down and there we wept . . .
> On the willows there
>   we hung up our harps . . .
> How could we sing the Lord's song
>   in a foreign land? (Psalm 137)

There in the shanty towns around the edge of the great Babylonian cities where they were forced into service, God's people struggled in the depths of grief and despair. We can imagine them telling and retelling what had happened, sifting through the fragments for some meaning, struggling to express faith in what felt like a deep void. Their belief in God had collapsed; they had lost identity, meaning and purpose. They were living as aliens in a foreign land and struggling to find hope in a world ruled by irresistible powers. There is something very contemporary about this crisis.

In the midst of all this a story began to emerge. Who told it first? When was that famous opening line first heard? Perhaps it was sung or chanted. The translation retains a sense of regular rhythmic pattern it may have once had:

> When God began to create . . . the earth was a formless void and darkness covered the face of the deep.

The song proceeds on a fourfold cycle, day by day . . .

> God spoke
>   And it was done
>   There was evening and morning
>   It was very good.

Where the exiles gathered, in times of prayer and worship, this song began to take hold of their imagination. There was something therapeutic in its rhythmic cycle; a firm and strong affirmation. It spoke to their longings and hopes. It was a gift for a people in dereliction and despair. The story was not told to explain some distant past. What use was that? It was told to minister to the present – to awaken new faith and to build up hope. As this song of creation unfolds, verse by verse, a new and powerful vision of God and his relationship with his world emerges.

Something from nothing

In the midst of their despair they hear of God, who has not abandoned them. Nor has he been defeated by the powers. He continues to create now as he did in the beginning. He can make something new out of absolutely nothing. He will bring new order and meaning out of what feels like chaos and destruction. He is secure. Chaos is not a threat to him. He is not in competition with it. He does not need to conquer it. His creation of humanity is still the place in his creation where his own likeness and being are expressed in a unique way. This God can be trusted despite present evidence and the experience of chaos and abandonment.

Called into life

In a world apparently abandoned to the brutal, impersonal will of earthly powers this story tells of a God who personally imagines and calls creation into being, in love and delight. The imagery is intimate and maternal. God brings the world to birth. The creating wind of the Spirit is described as 'hovering' over the deep. It is not an impersonal power that sweeps over the void. The word is used elsewhere to describe a mother bird, wings outstretched and fluttering over her brood. It also describes the movement by which the eagle provokes its young out of the nest to begin to fly.

The invitation to be

And when this awesome Creator God speaks, *'Let there be'*, what tone of voice do you think he is using? Is this the imperious command of an all-powerful ruler, demanding that his absolute will be done? Or is he choosing from infinite possibilities – 'How about . . . ?' Has God decided yet what he will make? Some suggest the phrase 'Let there be . . .' is like a word of gracious release – permission to be. Unlike worldly authority that dominates and forces us into submissive obedience, God invites the world into being. Life is given to itself. Creation is given its freedom. God does not impose his order on the world. Things are left remarkably open. There are no induction courses on gardening, animal care or prayer. Adam and Eve are not given a job description except in the most general terms: 'Go forth . . . be fruitful.' The working out of what that means day by day seems to be left to the creatures to decide. Life is possible, not prescribed. Faithful living is found in freedom.

> The 'Be fruitful' of God is answered not because of coercion but because creation delights to do the will of the Creator. Yet in the very closeness of trust, there is a distance that allows the creation its own freedom of action. Creation is not over-powered by the Creator. The Creator not only cherishes his creation but honours and respects it according to its own way in the relationship. The grace of God is that the creature whom he has caused to be, he now lets be. God lets creation create itself.[3]

The companionship of creation

Creation has its own life in God. It was around long before humanity appeared. This is a neglected insight. The human relationship to creation has all too easily been expressed in terms of domination, control and therefore exploitation. But though the relationship of humanity to God becomes troubled and painful, the Bible pictures the life of creation as a joyful celebration. The participation of all created beings in the worship of God is a constant theme in the Bible. Mountains, trees, animals, moon and stars all join in the praise of God. The sheer wonder of what is made awakens awe and prayer. 'The heavens are telling the glory of God', declares Psalm 19. Creation is pouring out a torrent of secret praise, night and day, never heard, 'yet their voice goes out through all the earth' (Psalm 19.4). The New Testament describes creation groaning in longing with all humanity for the fulfilling of life that was always God's intention (Romans 8.22). In Christian worship creation is never just a visual aid to provoke human worship. We are in joyful partnership – we call each other to the praise of God.

The world is a hidden sacrament, waiting to be revealed. The story is told of Thomas Merton in his hermitage, who burnt his supper one night during a storm because he was so captivated by listening to the rain talking. 'Think of it: all that speech pouring down, selling nothing, judging nobody'. I remember laughing for joy when I read it. I knew exactly what he meant, though nothing in my Christian inheritance had ever suggested such a relationship with creation was possible, let alone to be encouraged. Love for God awakens our love for all that he has made.

The companionship of creation was an unexpected comfort during the time in the Alps I have already mentioned. I was in a fragile state. On one occasion I had spent a long while weeping, feeling lost and frightened in the mystery of the pain and struggling to find God in it. After a while the tears stopped and I became still with a mixture of numbness and heightened sensitivity that can often follow an outpouring of grief. I became aware of my small log stove behind me. There in the corner of the room it crackled and clunked while the leaky old kettle on top hissed and steamed. It felt like a wise old friend who loved and understood but would not intrude upon this moment by coming nearer. I became aware of the bare plank walls of my cabin around me. They felt supporting, secure and sheltering – but without closing in upon my space. I looked out of the window. I watched the alpine grasses blowing in the meadow, the clouds tugging at the mountain tops, and felt the cooling air of the approaching evening. Everything around me seemed to understand. Without mocking or excluding, they all knew a secret. All this was sustained in love. All shall be well.

Everything in the garden

It is the children's bedtime and we are looking through a new Bible Picture Book. It starts with the Garden of Eden. My heart sinks. Any parent knows the struggle to say something intelligent about pictures and text that are either hopelessly sentimental, plain wrong, or reduce the mystery of creation to a predictable, dull moral tale. There are few more misused and abused corners of the Bible than the creation stories. We feel guilty because the Bible is the 'Word of God' and for Christians it *ought* to be alive with meaning.

That ancient story actually introduces us to a world that is excitingly open, pregnant with God's creative presence and full of enticing possibilities. To be made in the image of a God of

such unendingly creative imagination is to find our own vocation as explorers and adventurers rather than employees of a
huge wildlife park or landscape gardeners. But these illustrations
reveal just how hard we find it to tell these stories with any real
imagination. As a result they are powerless to awaken a vision
that might seriously turn our world around and even change the
way we live in it.

In the foreground an (apparently vegetarian) tiger is strolling
past a sleeping lamb ('Why isn't he eating it, Daddy? Isn't he
hungry?'). The rest of paradise is densely populated with similarly lethal combinations of species. Overhead the trees are
groaning with fruit.

In the background, Adam and Eve stand naked (lightly tanned
Caucasian), under the shade of an apple tree (is sunburn a risk
in paradise?). Though the story says they were 'naked and not
ashamed' the children's book illustrator arrives just as they have
walked behind a shrub with unusually wide leaves.

They are always just standing around in these picture books.
They look vaguely content, smiling in their innocence, but as if
they are waiting for some instructions to arrive. After all, what
is there for a gardener to do in a perfect garden? Without
corruption there will be no weeds. Without death there will be
no leaves to rake. What kind of dominion do they need to
exercise in a creation so benignly ordered and complete?

Even without the terrible fact and consequence of sin it is
hard to imagine a world in which there is genuine freedom to
explore, to grow, to learn, to make choices, to hope for and enter
into relationship with all that is made – unless there is also the
experience of struggle, pain, confusion, loss, failure – and even
chaos.

We are left with a story that is definite and heavy on God's
power, choice and will, but has very little vision of what human
beings are for – except as creatures made for obedience and
who, at first attempt, get it horribly wrong.

The children quickly sense there is no excitement to be found
in this garden and turn over to 'David and Goliath' or 'Daniel in
the Lions' Den'. I confess I am glad to follow them.

CHAPTER 4

Where the wild things are
Chance, order and freedom

> He must
> have chaos
> within him
> who would
> give birth
> to a
> dancing
> star.

THE NIGHT that Max wore his
   wolf suit
and made mischief of one kind
   and another,
his mother called him 'WILD
   THING!'
And Max said, 'I'LL EAT YOU
   UP!'
So he was sent to bed without eating
anything.

That very night in Max's room a forest grew
   and grew –
   and grew until his ceiling hung with vines
   and the walls became the world all around
   and an ocean tumbled by with a private boat for Max
   and he sailed off through night and day
   and in and out of weeks
   and almost over a year
   to where the wild things are . . .

Where the Wild Things Are was a favourite book with my
children for a while. Night after night we would read it together,
anticipating that fantastic moment where Max confronted the
wild monsters that were threatening him with those two words
(that we shouted aloud with Max) – 'BE STILL!' And then Max
tamed them 'with the magic trick of staring into all their yellow
eyes without blinking once. And they made him king of all the
wild things.'[1]

The Gospel of Thomas

By complete contrast their other favourite reading was a large edition of *Thomas the Tank Engine* stories. So from exploring the dangerous and exhilarating life-skills of managing monsters, we entered a benignly ordered world of talking steam engines. The Revd W. Awdry wrote his adventures of Thomas in the England of the early 1950s, in a society rebuilding life after the ravages of World War Two. The stories commend the importance of hard work, respect for authority, social considerateness, self-denial, and team effort for the common good.

This was an age when an efficient and newly nationalised railway system offered a metaphor for life itself. A very clear theology of God and creation is suggested in these stories too. In this world everyone knows his or her place. The natural ordering is hierarchical and patriarchal, from the superior (male) locomotives to the shunters, the more refined (female) passenger carriages to the unruly goods trucks (which need firm handling). Life in this world runs on preordained lines by timetable. Everyone has a given role and responsibility. It is not their task to question it but to be faithful and obedient to it.

The God of this world is the Fat Controller and the hope of every engine is to hear him say: 'Well done, Thomas, you're a really *useful* engine!' God is in control. Each story is a moral vignette, warning what happens when any engines 'selfishly' try to assert themselves and do something 'silly'. It is always disastrous. They go 'off the rails', causing all sorts of trouble for everyone else. Order is always restored, though, and all is duly forgiven. 'Sorry I've been such a chump,' said Thomas. 'That's all right,' said the Fat Controller, 'but don't do it again.'

Between two worlds

Where the Wild Things Are was a very controversial book when it was published in 1963 in America. The outward reason was a concern that the vivid pictures of monsters would frighten children. The underlying anxiety was surely more to do with placing this gloriously anarchic story into the hearts and imaginations of young children in the first place. This is subversive literature!

Written only a decade after Thomas' adventures, Max's world

is an altogether more potent, risky and conflictual place in which to grow up. It is a story about creative growth through conflict. Max is testing his boundaries against the powers that constrain his choices. There is a battle of wills. Growing up in this world involves the risky engagement with conflicting passions and relationships. Life is wild. There are monsters to be negotiated.

A popular assumption about God in relation to his world is that he is firmly on the side of order – that his world-view is much closer to Thomas' than to Max's. If God is God then his work is to overcome the wild and untamed elements that threaten life. He makes all things subject to his will and purpose. Life is not random or chance. God is in control – all-mighty, all-knowing, all-seeing, all-powerful.

In our insecure world where we live in growing fear of chaotic powers this picture is very appealing. If there has got to be a God we want him to be a real one: firmly in charge. But this picture is much too simple and raises more questions than it solves.

The question 'why'?

In the novel *The Bridge of San Luis Rey*,[2] a monk happens to be passing an ancient bridge in Peru at the very moment it collapses, pitching five hapless travellers into the ravine below. Brother Juniper believes that God orders and determines everything that happens. Here is a chance to witness to God's ways. He determines to find out as much as he can about those who have died because that is where the explanation will be found for their fate. The result is a famous reflection on the place of order and randomness, chance and God, faith and unbelief.

The book was quoted by Tony Blair at a memorial service for the victims of the terrorist attacks of 11 September 2001. The enormity of evil on that day raised questions for many people about why, if God is God, he did not prevent it from happening. He is all-powerful and all-knowing – he must have foreseen it and yet not acted.

But as individual stories emerged there were also disturbing events that, in less sinister contexts, we might call 'chance'. A man was late for work in the South Tower that day because his son was starting a new school and he wanted to take him. He lived. A woman went to work earlier than required that day because she was a caterer in the North Tower. She loved her work and wanted to give special care to a reception she was hosting later that day. She was killed.

If God is all-mighty and all-determining, was he really selecting individuals and nudging their schedules one way or the other, to life or death?

The truth is that this world can feel terrifyingly random and chaotic and (apparently) undefended by God. There is no evidence that wherever lives are facing catastrophe, whether as a consequence of human sin or as the work of unrestrained evil, that God's policy is to step in and stop it. 'God is in control' is a phrase that should only be uttered with great care. In fact the way the Bible actually speaks of God's relationship with this world is much more subtle.

Where the wild things are

This is well illustrated by a third creation 'story' in the Bible. It is actually longer than the two in Genesis but is hardly ever discussed alongside them. It comes at the end of the book of Job. After the long, desperate saga of Job's sufferings and the exhaustive attempts to find an explanation for them, chapters 38 to 42 contain God's magnificent and dramatic 'answer' to Job out of the whirlwind. Two long speeches follow.

The first is a beautiful poetic celebration of creation, from the song of the morning stars and the joyful shout of heaven as the foundations of the earth were laid, to the hawk on the wing and the mountain goat giving birth. But the second speech is an extended celebration of the creation of two wild, mythical creatures – Behemoth and Leviathan. In ancient Near Eastern religion these terrifying monsters represent the uncontrollable, chaotic forces of anti-creation and anti-God. They personify the archetypal human fear of the random element in life, and the constant anxiety that life may fall back into primordial chaos and non-being.

In some of the psalms, the chaos monsters are portrayed as arch-opponents of God's purposes. God does battle with them. Psalm 74.12 celebrates the power of God in overcoming and crushing Leviathan. God is greater than the mighty ocean and the untamed creatures within. The book of Revelation looks forward to a time when all these chaotic elements, personified by 'the dragon' or 'serpent', will be finally overthrown (Revelation 20.2, 10).

But here in Job, Behemoth and Leviathan are part of what God gave birth to in the beginning. 'Look at Behemoth which I made just as I made you,' he says to Job (40.15). He even describes his creation as 'the first of the great acts of God' (40.19).

God seems to find their existence exhilarating and even teases Job for his comparative frailty before them: 'Can you draw out Levia-than with a fish-hook?' (41.1). 'I will not keep silent concerning its mighty strength or its splendid frame . . . Who can stand before it?' (41.11, 12).

This is a long way from the benign, peaceful garden paradise of popular imagination. Here is a vision of a world that includes wild and untameable elements, beyond human strength to manage. God creates them just as he creates human beings. And though he clearly acts upon these forces, limits their destructiveness and on occasion overthrows them, he does not choose to remove them. The picture is ambivalent. These wild creatures are both exciting and threatening, part of creation and also destructive of it. But they are actually God's creation and celebrated as part of the gift of life. We are asked to hold strongly opposing elements in tension.[3]

A world of possibilities

If God has created wild and chaotic elements in life, our experience of living will always have a significant degree of uncertainty and unpredictability built into it. But this does not mean the world has been left entirely to chance. In these same speeches God also celebrates his ordering and shaping of life's rhythms and seasons. He is still Creator and God of all the world:

> Where were you when I . . . shut the sea with doors
> when it burst out from the womb? –
> and prescribed bounds for it,
> and said, 'Thus far you shall come, and no farther . . .'
> (Job 38.8, 10–11)

So the picture we have here is both more dangerous and more exciting. Order and chaos live in some kind of dynamic tension.

And if chaos cannot be allowed to bring life to final disintegration, nor is order allowed to impose a total predictability on life. It is the tension between these two apparently opposing forces that makes freely chosen and creative living possible. If God really were a Fat Controller, ordering everything by his will, life would be a sterile, repetitive, mechanical existence. Equally, if everything were random and left to chance, life would have no pattern to give it meaning and purpose.

It comes as no surprise to find that research into the natural world has established the significant place of chance in the evolving shape of life. There is evidence that some evolutionary changes may be caused initially by spontaneous changes in the behaviour of creatures. Animals just act out of character. As life advances into more complex, intelligent forms, the place of chance is taken by conscious choice.

All to play for

Two contrasting experiences of life may offer a way of understanding the creative tension in the relationship between order and chance.

Imagine a game of football or cricket between two strong and well-matched teams. The date and time are arranged some time beforehand. The playing area is precisely marked out. The teams must abide by accepted rules and an official is there to ensure that happens. The length of the game is timed to the second. But that is where the ordering of the game must stop. The game itself begins with the toss of a coin (and in the case of cricket the whole match can turn on this). The enjoyment and challenge lies precisely in the uncertainty of the outcome. All things are possible. There is everything to play for.

The second example comes from the world of music. I confess that whenever I want to capture the exhilaration of what I imagine the kingdom of God is like, I listen to jazz. Jazz involves a very disciplined relationship between order and spontaneity. At the heart of the music is the acceptance of a certain ordering, a core tune or theme. Without that the music will disintegrate into a nihilistic mess. But with it, musicians are free to take off in wild and chaotic flights. The one enables the other.

What is perhaps less well known is that classical composers

like Brahms and Beethoven left wide spaces in their music. These cadenzas were left open for the inspiration of individual musicians. Over time, and in a western culture increasingly concerned to regulate and order with ever more precision, the spaces were frequently filled in. Where before there had been free space, the cadenza was now set in print. The wildness was tamed.

Stalking the wildness

The tension we experience with the outside world is also found within each of us. When we talk about being 'in two minds' over a choice or course of action we are often struggling with our own relationship between order and wildness, between safety and risk. Exactly where the tension or 'dangers' are felt to be is greatly shaped by our life story and the people and circumstances that have most shaped our world-view.

A friend who was training for ordained ministry in the Church of England hit a crisis over whether he could go through with it. As we talked around his questions and uncertainties I felt as if I were hearing two different Peters speaking. They were two sides of his personality. One had a tendency to accept passively and 'go along with' what other people (God, authority, friends) thought was right for him. This was the side of him that had taken him through ministry selection procedures and much of the formal side of theological college. As with many people, his experience of church had reinforced the belief that this was the voice God wanted to hear.

But there was another side to Peter that was starting to protest. 'Hang on. Where are you taking me? Did you ever ask me what I thought of this idea?' This side of him looked askance at the prospect of spending the rest of his life in a declining institution with ageing congregations constrained by the dead hand of conservative, inflexible hierarchy. This side wanted something wilder, more creative, adventurous and risky for Christ. Here was the attractive energy and passion that God surely had in mind when he called him into ministry.

These two sides of his personality needed to talk to each other. His believing needed less order and more chance. He had to go stalking his wildness.

Call of the wild

It is well known that Charles Darwin's research into evolution contributed to his personal crisis of faith. As he observed the place of chance in the biological processes of developing life he had to question the prevailing belief in a Creator God. He struggled with church teaching of an omnipotent and omniscient God who ordered all things and allowed no room for the language of chance or for the honest ambivalence of those believers who wrote the story of Job.

Most of us are uncertain about how much we want life to be ordered anyway. The very quality that can make life feel frighteningly random and destructive can at other times make life a most exciting, energising and fulfilling experience. When life is exhilarating we would actually resent a God who kept stepping in to tell us the answers or make it safe without giving us the freedom to choose or to act out of our desires. Our dilemma is that when life overwhelms us we want a God to whom we can hand over the controls. God has created a world in which growing, exploring and developing involves living with elements of chance – of open possibility. God does not want to tame his world. We are called to wildness as much as to order.

We need to remember that the story in Job does not declare a world abandoned to chance (though it may feel like that at times). The presence of chance in the world does not mean that God has withdrawn from it. There is another possibility. What if he is to be found in the midst of life where choices are most real and possibilities at their most vital? What if this is God's way of calling us into life – attracting, enticing, tempting us to take risks and live more boldly? What if we are *drawn* to chance rather than abandoned to it?

In such a world life is both exciting and costly. Choices become more vital, human freedom more precarious and more imperative. Our greatest dilemma seems to be this: if we try to avoid the risks, we will miss the possibilities. There is no 'safe' living on offer.

The following prayer acknowledges the uncertainty and danger of our world. But significantly, it does not take refuge behind God, asking for his intervention. Rather, the prayer is for courage to live responsibly, fully and freely in the midst of life, where the wild things are, and so to be part of its transforming.

Saviour Christ,
in whose way of love
lies the secret
of all life
and the hope of all
people,
we pray for quiet courage to match
this hour.
We did not choose to be born
or to
live in such an age:
but let its problems challenge us,
its discoveries exhilarate us,
its injustices anger us,
its possibilities inspire us
and its vigour renew us
for your kingdom's sake.
Amen.[4]

CHAPTER 5

Undesirable Saviour
Jesus, the cross and the redeeming of love

> We are at one and the same time the beloved of God and the murderers of God.

WHAT IS IT about God's love that we must crucify it?

To be loved as God loves: nothing could be more desired – so nothing leaves us more vulnerable.

Nothing is more longed for – so nothing is more feared.

Our greatest struggle in this life is not with sin but with receiving the love with which God loves us.

It is love, not sin, that lies at the heart of the cross.

This is not a comfortable thought. However honestly we own our capacity for hating and hurting, we like to believe that our attempts at 'loving' come from a more innocent, well-intentioned part of ourselves. But we will not understand the cross until we face our ambivalence in love. Good Friday starkly reveals that love is a matter of life and death for us. Nothing is more important. Everything is at stake.

The real cross

The cross is usually thought of as the place where our badness is dealt with. The death of Christ is the terrible consequence of human sin. And it is about these things. But that is not where the story begins. The judgment of human sin is not the starting-place of God's action in the world. The well-known verse in John's Gospel reads, 'God so loved the world that he gave his only Son' (John 3.16). The text does not say, 'God so judged the world that he required punishment and death.' God was not compelled or required to act as he did. The cross is a gift of divine love.

When this idea is suggested in discussion groups, some people react strongly. The language of love is heard as a soft option. It is not tough enough. Humanity is sinful and under judgment. The world needs a drastic solution. 'The gospel is getting watered down,' said one person angrily. 'We must challenge people with the *real* cross – we must tell it like it is.'

But our own experience suggests that there is nothing soft about receiving love. It can be the hardest thing to do. Why do we pretend otherwise? A conference of counsellors and spiritual directors was asked, 'What is the most common area of struggle you meet in the people who come to see you?' They immediately replied – 'Being loved.'

But what people *say* they need is often quite different. When people come asking for spiritual direction (or help in finding a director) I always ask, 'What are you hoping to find in this relationship?' The replies are nearly always the same: 'I want someone to be accountable to', 'I want someone who won't let me mess around', 'I want someone who will challenge me and be tough with me when I need it'. The determination to develop a disciplined and mature Christian life is always impressive. But love is never mentioned. And God is love. Why do people assume that what they need more than anything, to grow close to God, is tough, firm handling?

Loved to destruction

Nothing lays bare the raw surface of our hungers, hopes and longings more than the gift of love. We are never more vulnerable than in the struggle to receive it. Even our most joyful encounters with love tell us this. When a friend fell deeply in love with the woman he would eventually marry he found himself swinging between joy and terror at what had suddenly come into his life. He knew he loved her. His terror was that *she* apparently loved *him*! 'I can't understand what she sees in me. It's frightening. She can't possibly know me. What will happen when she finds out? I'm afraid that when she does see the real me she won't love me any more.' He was a man who was outwardly confident and secure. He was forced to admit just how much his own sense of acceptance and belonging was normally sustained by his own efforts, and involved elaborate defences. And now something had got behind all those controls with a love that made them redundant. He was being offered a free gift.

There is a sense in which every gift of love is also a work of destruction.

The shaping of desire

We like to think that love is instinctive. Love is blind. It is beyond our control and leaves us helpless. We *fall* in love. But is it true? Of course it can awaken hugely powerful responses in us. But precisely what we love and find desirable is actually learned from watching those around us. The earliest patterns of children's play illustrate this process at work.

Two children are happily absorbed playing on a floor that is littered with toys and games. One starts to play with another toy. The other child (who has been happily playing with something completely different) sees this choice and suddenly desires that toy too. No matter that they had lost interest in it months ago: nothing else will do. War breaks out! To anyone watching it is clear that the rivalry is not really for the toy itself but for what it signifies. The child desires the toy because it is desired by another.

This is played out in adult society too. We experience desire in competition. We are rivals for love. We fight to secure a significant identity by claiming the desire of others for ourselves. All of this means that our places of security, loving and belonging are achieved by excluding others. To have an identity of my own I must have something that others do *not* have. To know myself loved and significant I must be part of a group that others are *not* part of. Thus *my* sense of personal love and worth is secured by excluding *you*. Indeed, it requires it. We are nurtured in a society in which the loving, desiring and identity that we crave for our human flourishing is founded on compulsive rivalry and exclusion. And it goes without saying that a huge and sophisticated advertising industry thrives on exploiting our anxieties by stimulating constant comparison.

This is exactly where the Bible locates the root of human sin. Adam and Eve are in a garden that is free and full of wonderful things to choose from and enjoy. They are told that one place alone in the garden belongs exclusively to God. Sure enough, that makes it particularly fascinating. They look on the tree that is God's and find 'it is to be desired' (Genesis 3.6). They steal the fruit from it. Their tragedy is that they simply cannot find the security to live with the possibility that something desirable belongs to someone else. The possibility that the other person might freely choose to make a gift of it is not considered. They have to have what God has. They have 'to be like him' (Genesis 3.5).

The gift of love

Now try to imagine what would happen if God were to enter a world like ours and live among us. How would we respond? What would happen?

God is love. But he is secure in that love and so he is free. He is not in competition with us or with anything he has made. No rivals threaten him. He does not need our love to fill any personal need of his. He has no insecurity that requires him to establish his identity by excluding anyone else. God's love is therefore an unconditional gift. It is completely *gratuitous* – the word means 'freely, spontaneously given, granted without favour or merit – without good grounds or cause'. He even loves without requiring any guarantee or assurance of how we will respond or what we will do with it. His love is genuinely disinterested and detached. Without any need to take us over or compel us into a response, it leaves us free to choose to love in return.

This is the love revealed in the coming of Jesus. The first thing that happens is that the world simply doesn't recognise him: 'He was in the world, and the world came into being through him; yet the world did not know him' (John 1.10). He finds himself a stranger in a world where life is founded on a totally different understanding of love and desire. The two languages have nothing in common. It is a complete clash of cultures. As he begins to reveal himself, his presence deeply divides people, so the stories and parables of Jesus often explore the needs and assumptions of two very different groups of people in his audience.

He told one story 'to some who trusted in themselves that they were righteous and regarded others with contempt' (Luke 18.11). A Pharisee and a tax collector arrive at the same time to pray in the temple. The Pharisee prays a prayer of pride: 'God, I thank you that I am not like other people, thieves, rogues, adulterers, or even like this tax collector. I fast twice a week and give a tenth of all my income.' Notice his confidence in himself and God is based entirely on his ability to exclude others. Because he is not like them, he knows he is special. His 'goodness' requires the exclusion of others who can be called 'bad' – for example that tax collector over there (as if God needs a visual aid at this point!).

By contrast the tax collector is a despised, unlovable outsider. Many hearers of the story would have been surprised at the idea that tax collectors prayed at all. 'Tax collector' and 'sinner' are almost synonymous in the New Testament. This man has nothing with which to offer or entice God's favour and he knows it. If God decides to be merciful to him it will be an entirely free gift outside of any deserving or means of gaining favour. His whole demeanour suggests little hope that his prayer will be heard: 'Standing far off, he would not even look up to heaven, but was beating his breast saying, "God be merciful to me, a sinner."' The scandal or delight of the story – depending on which group you belonged to in the audience – was that the tax collector was the one whose prayer was answered and went home loved.

No one in church Bible-study groups ever chooses to identify with the Pharisee in this story. But the damage done by religious rivalry is evident everywhere. The temptation to find our religious security by comparison, judging and excluding others is as powerful and destructive today as it was in the world of the Pharisees.

I remember to my shame a time when I met someone whose behaviour had caused deep hurt to close friends of mine. His actions had become public and he was now struggling to come to terms with what he had done. He was very penitent. For our part we had all told him we loved and forgave him. He found this even harder to take. It would have been easier to cope with if we had judged and shut him out. I sat with him, listening to turmoil, encouraging him of God's forgiveness and ours. But as I did so I became aware, with uncharacteristic honesty, that I was actually enjoying his discomfort and my role as forgiver and comforter. Being able to minister God's love to him was making me feel full of heroic Christian virtue and righteousness.

I remember sitting there, speaking the Christian words of comfort to him while inside a voice was saying: 'Well, it should hurt. It serves you right.'

The dilemma of love

Not surprisingly, those who found themselves outcasts from society, for whatever reason, welcomed Jesus with tears and joy. Women and men without the means to compete and establish themselves suddenly received all they longed for – quite unde-served. 'Love to the loveless shown that they might lovely be'. The stories are intensely moving but they caused social and the-ological chaos because Jesus ignored all the accepted boundaries of morality, holiness, goodness and badness.

If love is unconditional then all our goodness is actually irrelevant. I mean a 'goodness' that is founded on our anxious efforts to be desirable and secure, to the exclusion of others. Our goodness is no more a condition of being loved than our badness. Nor has love the slightest interest in any of the elab-orate mechanisms we devise to win its attention. 'Being good' is simply not the basis on which God chooses to know and love us.

For those who had succeeded in competing and establishing their good reputation that set them apart from other people, this revelation of divine love shook their very foundations. Jesus was quickly identified as a threat. Very soon they were plotting to destroy him (Mark 3.6).

Note that it was the good, devout, sincere people who cruci-fied Jesus. We miss the point entirely if we think that the cross is a consequence of our badness. The cross starkly reveals our problem with goodness. For Jesus, 'good' and 'goodness' were words whose meaning had become so polluted as to be unusable. When someone greeted him as 'Good Teacher', Jesus refused the word even for himself, insisting it could be applied to God alone (Mark 10.17).

So here we have it. In our flesh is revealed a way of loving and desiring that exposes a whole way of life for the manipulative rivalry that it really is. This love is so 'other' that it renders all our familiar techniques for finding and knowing love completely useless. What is offered is a totally new way of valuing ourselves. It is actually the love from which we came into being. And this is our dilemma: we can choose, in that love, to enter the turmoil of a radical conversion of life and faith, or we can choose to destroy it. The third outcome is the cross.

Enduring love

What can prepare us for the terror of being loved unconditionally? It means the worst in us has been accepted. We no longer have to hide and cover up what we find hard to love about ourselves. But however much we long for this to be true, it is something we instinctively fight against. We will be very ambivalent about whether we actually want this love at all. The risk may feel just too great. We have built defences around ourselves carefully and with reason. For those who have been deeply hurt, to be loved without condition can be barely endurable.

Jane had had a desperately painful childhood and her adult life had been a longing search for places to belong and be loved. None the less, she was a lively personality and had managed to put down roots quite quickly into a number of Christian communities over the years. But at regular intervals she seemed to need to destroy any loving relationships that had built up around her. Something in the nature of love was just too terrifying. It was as if the core of her own being was just too hurt to risk loving for any length of time. So at regular intervals, coldly and precisely, she would cut off the friendships of those closest to her and move on. In time, her search would begin all over again; the longing to be loved was always deeper than her fear of it. One of those on the receiving end said they had felt crucified. Jane cut off God too at such times, but through all her tortured wanderings a fascination and love for the person of Jesus would always return.

Surrounded by massive injustices, sustained violence and unrelenting innocent suffering, our talk of the cross needs to be more than neat legalistic equations about sin, guilt and acquittal. It is, first of all, the place of God's loving identification with the victims of his world. It is the measure of how tirelessly, and at what cost, God seeks to know and love us as we are.

This is not a knowing of us that sometimes finds expression in the thoughtless 'He understands how we feel, he's been here.' Has he? In what way? Did Jesus ever have a miscarriage? Was he ever raped or abused as a child? Did he watch his children die of starvation in a refugee camp? The identification is altogether deeper. On the cross, held by love not nails, Jesus is crucified into the hell that is the world's pain. He becomes the victim of victims. One Christian therapist, working with the most deeply damaged victims of life, would even speak of the cross as God's apology to them.

For one person this was a discovery that changed her for ever. Life had let her down bitterly, again and again. She felt unloved, victimised and full of pain. But there came a moment when something went wrong just once too often. Something snapped and this time she turned her full fury onto God. In her rage she imagined shouting and abusing Christ. She helped to crucify him, banging the nails into his hands and feet and shouting the anger of years into his face as he hung there. 'Now you know, now you know what it is like to live in a world like this!' Then came a moment when she realised Jesus was looking back at her. 'Yes, now I know,' Jesus said, in agony. 'Why else should I come?' As she looked at Jesus' contorted face she felt she recognised all her own wounds and struggles. It was a moment of conversion. The discovery that Jesus had descended into hell to share her pain and offer his friendship was the turning point of her life.[1]

The scapegoat

If the cross is God's place of willing identification with us it is also the place of our violent, wilful rejection of him. Jesus is made a scapegoat. Scapegoats are needed in any world where identity is founded on a basis as hopelessly insecure as competing desires. Scapegoats are the chosen victims on whom is laid the blame for those ills a society is unable to face about itself. The community can unite against the common enemy and can ignore, for the time being, the deeper anxieties about its own identity and motivation.

So at the fateful meeting of the Jewish authorities Jesus is correctly identified as a deadly threat to the present regime. The whole argument is based on competitive rivalry and envy. People are following *him* rather than *us*. 'If we let him go on like this, everyone will believe in him.' National security is invoked (always a useful argument for raising the stakes). Finally overriding waverers, the high priest declares – with classic scapegoat reasoning – 'it is better to have one man die for the nation than to have the whole nation destroyed' (John 11.47–50). Jesus is crucified for the common *good*.

But here is no normal scapegoat. In death, as in life, Jesus breaks the rules. Jesus lives in gratuitous love. He comes from completely outside any system of rivalry and exclusion. Nor can the system make any claim on him. He has committed no sin for which his suffering and dying is a consequence. Nor does he renew the cycle of violence by repaying it. Instead he forgives. Even his death is not part of any exchange. On the cross, divine love freely wills to indwell our humanity, enduring its chosen destiny to the tragic, bitter end. The moment he makes his death a free gift, the whole perverted system collapses. Something ends at the cross. That is why the New Testament writers often speak of the cross as the place where dividing walls and barriers of hostility are broken down (e.g. Ephesians 2.14).[2]

Learning to live in love

But even trying to speak of this is hazardous. Humanity is freely given an entirely new way of being. This is not a victory won at the expense of another who is defeated. Jesus has not taken one side rather than another. He is simply not part of the power struggles we assume to be the shape of human living. Even the sincerest language of 'debt' and 'owing' needs care. We simply cannot bring our familiar understandings of bad or good into the explanation. The whole system of human love, desire and valuing is what is being judged here.

Humanity is called to a completely new way of being and invited to begin again. The language of new birth is often used to capture the wonder and hopefulness of this conversion. But the task of living out this new identity is also like that of the stroke victim who, lost to every way of accustomed living, is now learning to speak and move again as if for the first time.

At the cross Christ brings us to a space in which we are free. We are given back to ourselves. And here we may begin our first faltering, vulnerable attempts to learn the way of love, desire and choice that in the life of God is perfect freedom.

CHAPTER 6

Ashes and kites
Sin, temptation, doves and serpents

> Be a sinner,
> and sin
> boldly, but
> trust and
> rejoice in
> Christ even
> bolder.

THE WORD 'temptation' simply means to be 'tested' or 'proved'. There is nothing wrong with that. It is not in itself sinful. Nor is it necessarily evidence of sinfulness – though it can cruelly expose our weakness of will and capacity for choosing wrong. The fact we are tempted at all is actually good news: temptation is the best evidence that we are alive! No one tempts the dead.

However frail we may feel in the face of it, temptation honours us with the assumption that we are free to choose and that our choices are real and important. Temptation is evidence of free will, of conscience and responsibility. It involves painful conflict because God has created a desirable world in which our choices matter, our actions have consequences and issues are worth struggling over. It also testifies to our freedom. Even what we call 'the Fall' is proof of how real human freedom really is. For we can only really love God because we are also free to refuse him. Thank God for temptation.

Driven into temptation

All of which may sound recklessly optimistic. For in most Christian teaching temptation is associated with wrongdoing. It is to be avoided. To be tempted is to be tempted to *sin*. But the accounts of the temptations of Jesus in the wilderness suggest a different understanding.

The story begins with John the Baptist by the River Jordan,

calling people to repent of their sins and to prepare for the
coming of the Messiah. It is here that Jesus makes his first public
appearance and launches his earthly ministry. To John's astonish-
ment, Jesus' first words are to ask to be baptised along with
everyone else. Baptism was a sign of repentance – an acknow-
ledgement of lives that need washing clean. Only sinners need
baptism. Before any miracles or teaching, Jesus first identifies,
utterly and completely, with the world he has come to save. He
even enters its disorder and sin. 'For our sake he made him to be
sin who knew no sin' (2 Corinthians 5.21).

St Mark continues the story in typically direct and dramatic
style:

> Just as he was coming up out of the water, he saw the heav-
> ens torn apart and the Spirit descending like a dove on him.
> And a voice came from heaven, 'You are my Son, my beloved;
> with you I am well pleased.'
>
> And the Spirit immediately drove him out into the wilder-
> ness. He was in the wilderness forty days, tempted by Satan;
> and he was with the wild beasts and the angels waited on him.
> (Mark 1.9–13)

What is startling is the way the Spirit treats the newly baptised
Son of God. Jesus is 'driven' into the wilderness in the same
violent language that will shortly be used to describe the fate of
demons (Mark 1.15 and 25)! As often happens, the other
Gospels tone down Mark's bluntness. In Matthew Jesus is 'led
up by the Spirit' into the wilderness. If this sounds more like a
guided tour by comparison, the reason for leading him there is
made even more explicit – it is 'to be tempted by the devil'
(Matthew 4.1).

For those of us who regularly pray 'lead us not into temptation' this story is disturbing. Here we have the Holy Spirit
aggressively leading Jesus into precisely that. How are we to
understand it? Three things are immediately clear.

First, God seems to be in the business of temptation. He has
even apparently arranged an appointment for Jesus with the devil.

Second, temptation *follows* baptism and commitment to the
Father's will. Testing and temptation are a direct consequence
of baptism. It is not necessarily the weakness of faith or lack
of commitment it is easily assumed to be. Temptation may be

evidence of living, vibrant commitment to God. We are tempted because we are *more* alive, not less so.

Third, the temptations of Jesus are the consequence of being filled with the Spirit. His struggles in the wilderness are directly linked to the descent of the Spirit upon him. He is in the wilderness because the Spirit has forced him there. In the yearly cycle of scripture readings these stories are usually read during the season of Lent, where the emphasis is on the struggle against sin and the need for discipline. But they might equally be read in the season of Pentecost. Temptation can be a fruit of the Spirit!

The wilderness of the Spirit

If this challenges our expectation of where temptation may be coming from, it may also change our vision of the Holy Spirit. All four Gospels describe how the Spirit descended on Jesus at his baptism 'as a dove'. As if to stress this as a physical encounter rather than a figurative reality of this encounter Luke adds 'in bodily form' (3.22).

In his book *Wild Beasts and Angels* Michael Mitton questions the significance of this and offers some unexpected insights.[1] Down the centuries Christian art has traditionally portrayed the descending Spirit in this scene as a small, delicate, pure white dove. But that is not the kind of dove that is described there. The Greek word describes a rock dove. This bird is neither immediately striking nor attractive. It looks like an ordinary English woodpigeon. Rock doves like rocky and rugged desert terrain. They make their homes in inhospitable and hostile places where human life would instinctively feel under threat and at risk. This is the bird that mysteriously appears overhead and descends on Jesus as he emerges from the water.

If the Holy Spirit should choose this bird to embody his life and character it is not surprising to find that the one who receives it is compelled to enter the wilderness that is its natural habitat. Far from offering protection from the raw dilemmas of human life and choice, the Holy Spirit is found to be a tough provoker and tester of life. He risks leading us closer to the vulnerabilities that surround our conflicting desires. In his presence our desires, longings and choices are not lessened, but become more vivid, more vital.

So temptation does not just leave us in danger of evil and

sin – we are even more in danger of God. In the wilderness of testing, we not only meet the burden of our own sinfulness for what it is, but we are also driven by the power of God towards our redemption and transformation. If there are temptations to resist, there are others to give in to. The untamed wilderness Spirit is at work tempting us to choose life, to risk growing in grace, to surrender to the adventure of faith. The struggle is real and may take us to our limits, but it is one that God will actually provoke for his own ends: so we may choose, if we will, to be strengthened and liberated.

Doves and serpents

When Jesus sends his disciples into the world he calls them to be 'wise as serpents and innocent as doves' (Matthew 10.16). These two qualities are not easily pictured together. How can you be wise *and* innocent? And don't snakes eat birds? The older form of the ordination service asked God to 'adorn' those who are being made priest 'with innocency of life'. But I have yet to find any prayers asking God for snake-like cunning! Aren't we missing something here?

We should by now be wary of assuming we know what qualities Jesus has in mind when he calls us to innocence! The word usually describes a state of undefiled pre-experience. It is a form of virginity, and like virginity, it cannot be restored once it is lost. We speak of the supposed 'innocence of childhood' in this way. It can only be preserved pure and intact through avoiding those conflicts and experiences that might taint or corrupt its virginal goodness.

But the innocence that Jesus speaks of is clearly quite different. It is learned; and to learn it requires the contradictory virtue of serpent cunning. Jesus calls his followers to an open-eyed and canny understanding of the world; one that can only come from a full and vigorous involvement in it. Snake-like wisdom is not for fooling. It sees life as it really is – with all its capacity for duplicitous evasion and outright evil. Christian innocence lies in learning to live by a way of responding that leads to our transformation rather than our corruption. It is costly and risky, but it is the way that leads to life.

In the first instance it simply requires honesty in the face of questions. But this is not an area where Christian ministry lives very comfortably with its task. In a church where I ministered I decided to broaden the traditional confirmation classes to make them more exploratory and enquiring. The next Sunday I advertised them, off the cuff, as 'a kind of Agnostics Anonymous'. The interest was immediate and the name stuck. For the next few years I ran several groups each year. It attracted people from outside faith who wanted to understand it better, as well as long-term church members who kept saying that here was a place they could ask questions they had not felt able to ask before. We had two ground rules: 1. Every question is valid; 2. You do not have to become a Christian at the end of it.

As the leader I was surprised by how uncomfortable I found the groups. I had to lose control of the process. Until that moment I had not seen just how formulaic my approach to teaching and discipling actually was. I had been passing on what I myself had received. But my well-intentioned (though anxious) concern to encourage clear and confident faith tended to be prescriptive rather than open. The atmosphere was protective rather than adventurous. Answers were given *before* the questions. All too easily this could lead to a faith pursued apart from life. Selective non-engagement with the hostile and troubling 'world' is often encouraged as a faithful response to believing.

But in the groups it was the questions that were life-giving. Time and again people emerged with deeper and more authentic relationships to God and to their own lives. People actually came to life in the questions – and so did God!

Since there is no way of withdrawing completely from issues, questions and dilemmas, people can find themselves trying to sustain two lives. Where this tension is most clearly revealed is in the inability of many church communities to relate Sunday faith creatively to the weekday world of work and society. One person spoke of it as a double pain. She had a costly commitment to work that kept her in the front line of complex moral and social issues, to which there were often no clear answers. But she experienced her church community happily worshipping and praying in what felt like a parallel universe. Her call to struggle in the wilderness was not supported or even understood for what it was.

David Martin adopted exactly this bold strategy when, as a young Christian, he became a student at the London School of Economics. It was an aggressively secular institution at the time.

He was the only Christian in his department and he came from a fundamentalist Methodist background. 'I exposed myself deliberately to as much contrary thinking as I could, in order to work out a position . . . I stood at the crossroads and took whatever came. I suppose it is the most Christian thing I've ever done.'[2] This is nothing less than risky faithfulness to the wilderness of the Spirit.

Today he continues to be known as a firmly committed Christian and one of the world's most eminent sociologists. He argues that two convictions lie at the heart of the Christian witness in the world: a belief in the power of the gospel to transform life; and an uncompromising sense of the iniquity of evil. The hope of the gospel is found precisely in the place that most threatens it. You cannot have one without the other. A world-view dominated by evil will lead to withdrawal, hopelessness and despair. But a gospel without a shrewd discernment of the reality of evil will degenerate into the ineffectual 'happy consciousness' that he fears is infecting the Church in its desire for relevance and growth. In the moment when, for our salvation, we are being driven into the wilderness, our temptation will be to spend our time building amusement arcades.

Real sins

In one of Graham Greene's novels, a priest is sitting in a confessional listening with growing impatience to the familiar litany of petty grudges, minor infringements and the familiar preoccupations of sterile devotion. He loses his temper and snaps, 'Why don't you confess your *real* sins?' The penitent looks up at him in blank incomprehension. Greene's priests are better advertisements for whisky than pastoral practice, but here the question goes to the heart of the matter.

The strategy of the devil in the wilderness is very revealing. The temptation was not primarily to wrong actions or misuse of personal power. Jesus was tempted to doubt his own identity. Again and again the devil attacks the roots of his personal security: 'if you are the Son of God . . .' (Matthew 4.3 and 6).

When we define sin solely in terms of wrong actions or thoughts, we trivialise it. Our diagnosis does not go deep enough. The problem is more radical and fundamental. Jesus furiously castigated and mocked the religion of his day for its pedantic obsession with external standards of behaviour. Who we are always comes before what we do. Our choices, desires and actions will always flow from our sense of personal identity. Our deepest need is not primarily to stop doing or saying bad things. The power and significance of sin lies not so much in what we are doing or saying, but in who we think we are.

Real sin – the sin that is still Original to this world – is at root an insistence on being what we are not – a desire for a life other than the one we are given. So it is ultimately the pursuit of a world that does not exist. This way of life unfolds as a helpless and tragic case of mistaken identity.

When tempted, Jesus refused to act for short-term satisfaction, to seek special privilege or build an empire through alliance with the powers. He ruggedly affirmed his identity and security in the will of the Father alone.

Friend of sinners

To find Jesus struggling in the wilderness of human temptation, of all places, is what makes the Christian faith so uniquely hopeful.

First, because we find him where we are. God is with us. He knows in his own being our struggles and our compulsive waywardness. In fact he knows them better than we do. Only someone who has never given in to temptation can know its full power. The New Testament writers are emphatic that he was offered no privileged protection. He was not an all-powerful Superman hiding behind the pretended weakness of the bumbling Clark Kent. Rather, 'he was tempted just as we are yet without sin' (Hebrews 4.15). His victory was won in a situation that is identical to ours – except that it was tougher.

Second, because to those battered and wearied by the struggles they face, Jesus offers his presence as comfort and companionship. 'Come to me, all you that are weary and are carrying heavy burdens and I will give you rest' (Matthew 11.28). 'Because he was tested by what he suffered, he is able to help those who are being tested' (Hebrews 2.18). Throughout history, Christians facing all kinds of trials and difficulties have found hope and comfort in this realisation.

Third, because there is hope for sinners. Right there, in our failure and guilt, we may discover the most unexpected gift of all – the mercy, forgiveness and friendship of God. We find ourselves held in our frailty, prayed for in our immaturity, sought out and guarded despite our infinite appetite for distraction and wandering off. Only those who have reached the limit of themselves, with nothing to offer in their own defence, fall into the abyss of love. In fact only sinners understand the gospel. It is not available to anyone else.

St Paul speaks of it as a 'putting off' and 'putting on'. It suggests to me being able to shed, at long last, some bulky old clothes that I have worn as long as I can recall. I now see them for what they are. They never really fitted. They were not 'me' at all but they were all I had to wear. And instead I am now trying on something that seems to be absolutely made for me – or rather that I was made for. I am, at last, becoming who I really am.

Ashes and kites

By ancient tradition, at the beginning of Lent, Christians receive the sign of ash on their foreheads. As they do so they hear the sober words, 'Remember you are dust and to dust you shall return; repent and believe the gospel.' Ashing is a universal symbol of human mortality, of grief and mourning for sin, and of penitence. This is a season for serious reflection and for practising the disciplines that strengthen the fight against everything that denies Christ. Christian living is to be marked by watchfulness, careful self-examination. There are tears to be shed. There is no cheap grace. It is the way of the cross. The three promises made at baptism must remain the foundation of our living: 'I turn to Christ; I repent of my sins; I renounce evil.'

But there is another symbol for this season – a complementary one. Some Greek Orthodox communities mark the start of Lent in a quite different way. For them the first day of Lent is treated as the first outdoor day of the new year. Lent is the beginning of spring. After the long death of winter, here is the first sign that new life is coming. We must go out to greet it. The community celebrates this day by climbing the nearest hill and flying kites on the fresh spring wind!

Always more important than what we turn *from* is what we turn *to*. Here we meet the Spirit enticing, provoking, driving, inspiring us in the struggle to turn from our bondage to a useless evil, to live boldly and be caught up into the adventure of divine love.

CHAPTER 7

In the will of a willing God
Guidance, providence and the mystery of things

> Love –
> and do
> what
> you wish.

A MAN was wandering through the heat of the desert. He seemed to be looking for something. His name was Macarius and he would become one of the founding saints of the Egyptian Coptic Church. His problem was that he knew God was calling him to build a monastery, but he did not know where. He searched the wilderness asking God to show him the right place to build it. 'Give me a sign'. 'Show me'. 'Is it here – or over there?'

But God was silent.

At last, after another day filled with fervent prayers for guidance an angel appeared with a message from God: 'The Lord is not going to show you where to build the monastery. He wants you to choose the place. If he tells you where to build and things go wrong, you will only blame him. So you must choose.'

Surprised by choice

God's answer is unexpected. This is not the way guidance is supposed to work, is it? The Lord's Prayer clearly tells us to pray '*your* will be done'. And surely personal freedom and choice are to be surrendered to God? 'You make your own mind up' is not usually the challenge at the end of Christian testimonies of doing God's will.

Nor are we used to thinking of God's will as something so permissive that it leaves much up to us. This may not even be the kind of God we were hoping for. The idea of a God who has lovingly preplanned our whole lives in detail is very appealing in such an uncertain and hazardous world. We would prefer a God who decides for us; who has the right job in mind for us; who has planned the right partner for us to marry; and so on.

Some might even question whether this is a Christian understanding of guidance at all. Did not Jesus say 'follow me'? Does not the Bible encourage us to believe that when we commit our way to God 'he will direct your paths'; or promise that 'your ears will hear a word behind you saying, "This is the way, walk in it"'? Does God guide our lives by his plan or not? But the true question is not whether God has a will, but what kind of will he has. How does he express it? The experience of Macarius points to four qualities of the will of God.

First, the story begins with the assumption that God has a will and plan. He also calls people to participate in the accomplishing of it. Human living is a vocation to live in God's will. Macarius clearly believed that. For him, being a Christian meant he should seek God's will and obey it as a matter of central priority in his life. He was a man passionately pursuing a strong sense of God's calling him to a certain project. This is not questioned. But God's is not an imposing, authoritarian will. Still less is it an impersonal command requiring absolute obedience regardless of the needs of the mortal beings who must carry it out. In a world where all-powerful wills are more often experienced as coercive and abusive of human dignity and freedom, this is unexpected and good news.

When Jesus teaches his disciples about what leadership involves he explicitly contrasts the absolute, overbearing will of secular rulers who 'lord it over' people, with the way power is exercised in God's kingdom. By utter contrast, God expresses his will in loving, self-giving service. Even Jesus did not come into this world to be served but to serve (Mark 10.42–45).

The sheer courtesy of God towards us is something little prepares us for. Surveying the range of human roles and jobs for comparison, God recognises himself more fully in the life of an earthly slave than in the status and power of an absolute ruler. It is not surprising if this is hard for us to adjust to. We may instinctively go on relating to him through the authoritarian, directive will we think God ought to have.

Second, God's will is not predetermined and inflexible. There is a divine plan but it delights to leave space within it. Human will, desire and action are to be an important and creative part of the fulfilling of it. Although God's will is clear in general terms (build a monastery), there is much more that has not been revealed (where to build it – and presumably a host of other practical details). At this point God goes silent. Macarius must make his own mind up, discern what is appropriate and serve God through his personal will and imagination.

Living in God's will does not mean receiving a 'perfect plan' package that we must simply unwrap and obey. Living in God's will does not mean being told what to do all the time.

Some approaches to guidance veer perilously close to this kind of belief. God is God. He knows everything. His will is perfect and, in the end, will be achieved with us or in spite of us. Taken to its extreme, human choice becomes meaningless, prayer pointless (and this book irrelevant). No action or decision can be taken, however small, without specific guidance to do so. Although God's love and human free will is stressed, we are little more than mildly animated puppets. God's will for Macarius is to give him his own will. And obedience to God's will requires him to enter a freedom of his own. To obey God is to be free.

In fact, human choice is a central concern of God in this story. So to be faithful to God and to the task, Macarius must use his own discernment and make a choice.

Third, the story warns us against a narrow understanding of what guidance is about. It is much more than making factually 'right' decisions about what God wants us to 'do'. His plan is not a blueprint: God shows no interest in the precise practical details here. His loving interest is focused on Macarius and the kind of person he may become as he fulfils God's purpose.

So guidance is not a technique to be mastered but life to be entered. The question 'What decision is God guiding to me to make?' is part of a much bigger and more important question: 'What kind of person is God willing that I may become?'

Finally, this is a vocation Macarius must freely choose. There are very practical, particular reasons given why this is important. God knows that if Macarius is to be faithful to his vocation when the going gets tough, it must be something that he has freely chosen. He must own it. This is shrewd pastoral leadership. Passive conformity can be confused with real faith, but it can never inspire the determination or endurance that faithful living requires.

Mountains and plains

When the subject of guidance comes up we usually turn to the clear and unambiguous examples in the Bible. We are encouraged to believe that if God guided Moses, Abraham and St Paul he will surely guide us too. True though it may be, it is a thoroughly intimidating comparison. But it can be unhelpful for another reason: because we are only focusing on the special, highly dramatic, supernatural stories. These are made the ideal: 'This is how God would always speak to us all the time if only we were more open and committed and sensitive to his Spirit.' But is that true?

In the Bible those stories are the exception not the rule. Nor does the Bible treat supernatural works of God as more important than his natural works. The splendour of the night sky or the rising of the sun is as much a revelation of God's glory as the parting of the Red Sea. The danger is that if we only expect God's presence in the exceptional, the dramatic and supernatural interventions, then we will not know how to find him in what is ordinary.

There is wisdom in the way the Jewish faith expresses this relationship. The festival of Pentecost celebrates the earth-shaking revelation of God at Sinai and the giving of the law. The account of that awesome encounter with God is read aloud during the worship. But the other reading is in total contrast. It is from the book of Ruth. You could have no greater contrast. Alongside the fire, thunder and overwhelming glory of God on the mountain we have – a story of two women and a farmer. In this story God is hardly even mentioned. He is not prayed to directly. He is not sought for guidance. He works no miracles. In fact for substantial periods he seems painfully absent. Only once, at the end of the story, is an event attributed to God's direct intervention.

In this story of a vulnerable human's journey back from tragedy to new beginnings, God's presence is unseen and certainly unrecognised. It none the less weaves a frail thread of redemption through day-to-day human choices, costly love and faithful loyalty and friendship.

The message is clear. The God of Sinai, the God of great, thunderous revelations and awesome theophanies, is the God of ordinary life. The revelation on the mountain top is worked out and expressed in the valleys – in the stories, joys and struggles of daily living. In the Bible God's will is often worked out through the very ordinary choices of God's faithful people. The more specific and direct guidance of God seems to come when his people need teaching, information or direction they could not otherwise discern.[1]

Willing life

So what is God's will for us? To live in the life he gives. Do we need to know any more than that? And the one who creates us also personally sustains the world, moment by moment, through his providential ordering. He exercises infinite and costly care upon the world. Not a sparrow falls to the ground without him knowing. 'In him we live and move and have our being' (Acts 17.28).

This means that the world is full of him. All things are alive in him. Jesus found signs everywhere of the Creator's character and love. 'Where can I escape from your presence?' cries the psalmist (Psalm 139.7). The whole earth is full of his glory. The world can only find fulfilment and purpose in a living relationship with God.

We are not talking about a vague force for good. In the Bible the idea of providence concerns a very specific trust in a God who makes promises and enters into committed relationships with people. Trust in his ordering is based on his own character, not on how things are actually turning out at any one moment.

Jesus reveals how much this sustaining can be marked by infinite suffering and pain-bearing. Even in the deepest desolation of life this love is present. 'Nothing can separate us from the love of God' (Romans 8.35). He is not overcome by the things that crush us. His will can be frustrated but never finally denied by the wilfulness of his world. He can bring new life even out of death itself.

This means that 'though the fig tree does not blossom, and no fruit is on the vine; though the produce of the olive fails and the fields yield no fruit'; though it looks on the surface of life as if God is completely absent, 'yet I will rejoice in the Lord; I will exult in the God of my salvation' (Habakkuk 3.17–18). So we seek God in the struggles and uncertainties of life. We search for him – as he searches for us.

Life is thin

The Celts have an idea of 'thin places'. These are places that seem to be more spiritually porous, where prayer is somehow easier and God's presence more real. What if life itself is thinner than we know or expect? Research has revealed a remarkably high percentage of people with no religious commitment who have received important experiences of sensing 'God', 'divine Spirit' or a 'numinous presence' at moments in their life. What is less well known is that these experiences are on the increase at the very moment that traditional church life is in steep decline. These moments are often marked by intense wonder, an awareness of a higher benevolent power, a sense of patterning and purpose to life, and comfort that a prayer out of distress has been lovingly heard. Most importantly, they happen in very ordinary moments of life.[2]

> I was three years old. I crouched down, as children do, very close to the ground. A black slug moved across the path, very slowly, silently, leaving a shiny trail, and I sat back on my haunches to watch it. My cotton print dress circled the ground around me. Overhead the sky was blue, the sun shone . . . a tune was in my head and I hummed it . . . There was a movement among the trees. Not the movement made by someone passing through but an overall rustle of attention as in a crowd before the arrival of royalty. Each leaf was aware, expectant. Each blade of grass alert. God was everywhere. I felt secure; held; at one with everything around me.[3]

Many of these stories have been remembered from earliest years but had never been shared before. This is significant. It may be partly a social inhibition. In my experience, where a person feels secure enough to share such a story in a church context they often start by saying, 'Of course, I know you won't agree with this but . . .' Official religion is expected to stand in judgment of their experience and find it wanting. It means that many people, finding their lives unexpectedly touched by signs of profound spiritual reality, never find a place where they can talk about it and discern the significance of what they received.

Spies of God

In the light of all this, what is guidance for? If Jesus is Lord of

all the world; if nothing separates us from his love; if his presence fills all things; does it matter what we do with our lives
exactly? Yes, because God wills it so. Yes, because we are part of
something infinitely bigger than ourselves, a partnership of life
so intricate and full of possibilities that we have scarcely begun
to imagine it. Yes, because we are part of a dangerously disordered and wilful world that is perilous without his wisdom,
unbearable without his compassion and unknown without his
joy. So our vocation is to become God's spies, seeking out the
clues, the signs, the fingerprints, the mind of God amid the
'strange, unknowable conspiracies of the world . . . a world full
of strange purposes and mysterious outcomes'.[4]

Let me suggest four starting principles for Christian guidance:

1 Life in God's will is a call to the fullness of life. We must
beware of making it a narrowly 'spiritual' task. It may be that
what best equips us to respond to the particular moments of
crisis of decision in our lives is how we live in the times
between.

I learned a lot from a colleague I once worked with. He was
always looking to broaden his experience of life. He was
interested in trying things he had never done before, meeting
people of different life-experience than his, and developing
his own Christian experience. It is partly a matter of temperament, but I noticed how relaxed he was about decision-making
and issues of guidance. He said his prayers and lived as widely
as he could.

2 Life in God's will is sustained and strengthened in the disciplines of regular prayer, worship, Bible-reading and listening
to God in the shared wisdom of God's people. As in the Bible,
God's will is to be discerned and lived in the community of
faith.

3 Life in God's will is not prescribed for us. There may be times
when God must guide us very specifically, but his desire is
always to open us to the dilemmas of choice and the struggle
for discernment. The right response to the question, 'Why do
I find it so hard to hear God's will?' may sometimes be 'Why
do you find it so hard to make decisions?' God's will calls us
to personal responsibility for our own decision-making.

4 A life in God's will means a willingness to live honestly in the
mystery of things. Trust in God is not in the guarantee of a

certain outcome so much as in his constant love turning all things towards the fullness that is his presence.

Simply because our questions matter so much we can easily misread or manipulate 'the signs'. I have known times when a decision felt charged with cosmic significance – but with hindsight it was nothing of the sort. Other decisions that appeared routine, and that could have gone either way, have proved life-changing – most memorably the sequence of events that led me to meeting my wife.

The sheer mystery of God, of life and of ourselves means that we offer our choices in a spirit of faithful agnosticism. Thomas Merton was a deep man of prayer, a passionate and adventurous pioneer of Christian living, but for all the vision that has made him such an influential writer, he still says:

> My Lord God I have no idea where I am going.
> I do not see the road ahead of me.
> I cannot know for certain where it will end.
> Nor do I really know myself,
> And the fact that I think I am following your will
> does not mean
> that I am actually doing so.
> But I believe that the desire to please you,
> does in fact please you.
> And I hope I have that desire in all that I am doing.
> And I know that if I do this
> You will lead me by the right road,
> Though I may know nothing about it.[5]

The sea of faith

There is one experience of guidance that I have never forgotten.

He was a man who led boat trips around an island off the coast of Wales. There was nothing he did not know about those waters. He was an endless source of information, yet it was not his knowledge that made such an impact on me so much as the way he knew and shared it with us. His was not the oft-repeated list of facts and stories that characterise many such tours. He spoke out of an intimate, living relationship to all around. There was a kind of fullness about him and in his presence everything around seemed more alive and interesting. He heard our questions with attentiveness and careful respect. His answers showed a loving reverence for what he was naming. He did not impose his knowledge on us – he rather offered an invitation into a way of life. With untroubled authority he handled the fierce currents and tides and all the while he lent us his eyes, his wisdom, his time and his deep love for all around him. His guidance felt like an invitation into life. And all I wanted was to follow him.

That is how God guides.

CHAPTER 8

You did not choose me,
I chose you

Choice and belonging in a consumer society

> And nothing
> more.
> A shambles
> of desire
> collapsing
> steadily in
> upon itself.

DID YOU KNOW that you blink more rapidly when approaching the checkout in your supermarket?

Were you aware that when you walk down a high street you speed up when you are passing a bank?

Have you noticed that the aisles in supermarkets that stock commodities of particular interest for women are wider than the others?

How does it feel to learn that just by looking in your bathroom cabinet and kitchen food cupboard a consumer researcher can fairly accurately predict what car you drive and where you spend your holidays?

We are never more closely observed in our western society than when we are making choices. A huge and sophisticated consumer research industry exists solely to predict, stimulate and manipulate our life choices in a world that it treats as one big market place. Its power lies in the fact that we live largely unaware of its impact on our living.[1]

A world to choose from

Choice is a contemporary obsession. To have ever-increasing choices and the means to indulge them is regarded as a definitive sign of a culture that is socially and economically thriving. To create and sustain such a world is the elusive goal of political life.

But choice today comes to us in a particular packaging. It is not value-free. The controlling market ideology requires the constant stimulation of choice without regard to actual need or desirability. This economy needs endless consumption to survive. More worrying still, there is no alternative on offer.

This was never more clearly reflected than in the weeks following the attack on the Pentagon and the World Trade Center in New York. At the time many people insisted that the shock of that event had changed their lives. The crisis had jolted them out of complacency and challenged them to ask what they valued most.

There was enormous political anxiety about the sudden decline in consumer spending that followed. Governments urged people to defy terrorism by showing that the western democratic way of life could not be overthrown. They worked feverishly to stimulate their economies and restore 'consumer confidence'. Spending is for them a sign that a nation is confident. By Christmas of that same year consumer spending in Britain had reached record levels. Retail purchasing that month alone equalled the government spending on health for that entire year.

Producer to consumer

Choice is not what it used to be. Our relationship to our world has fundamentally changed.

My parents were born, educated and socialised into a world that expected them to become responsible producers contributing to the progress and good of the whole. Whether or not religion was explicit in this vision, the words 'duty' and 'vocation' were understood and approved. They were taught the importance of saving. Thrift was a virtue. There was a belief that things were worth waiting for, that tomorrow was important and was shaped by the values and sacrifices of today.

By contrast my children are growing up in a world that requires them to be consumers. The central value of our society has moved from progress to choice. The consumer economy is a spending culture. The priority is today not tomorrow. There is little incentive to save. We live in the present regardless of tomorrow.

The result is that we are a society living way beyond our means. Currently, one in four adults have significant problems relating to debt and the level is rising. Western consumer society has institutionalised overspending without regard for the consequences.

Crisis of identity

There is a further consequence to this. Personal identity and belonging was once based on participation in a society that had some consensus about its defining vision and values. Community, tradition and shared meaning provided a framework within which I knew myself and explored my place and vocation in the world.

That social consensus has now collapsed. The very idea of citizenship is in crisis. We are all customers now. So shopping is now one of the few activities on offer where we can 'know ourselves' in some tangible way. My 'self' is no longer regarded as something given or revealed. We have to create it for ourselves. We are identified by what we buy, choosing our identities much as we choose the clothes we wear. And like clothes, the fashion constantly changes. So our sense of who we are is in a constant state of flux. We build up portfolios of identities each appropriate to the different contexts of our world. These 'identities' may have little relation to each other. Nor do we expect them to. Each is an attempt to cope with one of the shifting roles that make up our living. We shop in order to belong. The logo on our clothing defines our alliances and our status. Consumer choice is a choice about where we belong.

The cost of sustaining these manufactured selves is very high. We can only keep some kind of balance by a selective withdrawal of our real selves. We minimise personal involvement at any level of depth and develop a hard, defensive core around our inner world. Life is lived from the outside, on the surface and for the moment. Even the tenderest of human intimacies, by which we once knew ourselves to be in love, are now used for recreation. We are strangers to ourselves and to each other.

Our dilemma is the same as the Invisible Man. We have fallen into non-being. We are invisible to ourselves and each other. Lacking true substance we use our desires and choices to clothe and bandage our non-existence. Now at least there is something to be seen. We evade the terror of our emptiness by covering it up.[2]

The consumer market thrives on the needs of this empty self. But it can only offer a choice between strategies for distracting, or soothing, our superficial need. What is actually needed for fulfilment is another way of being.

Suffering from consumption

The social cost of this is more evident by the day. By any measure of social health, our current way of life is clearly bad for us. Social analysts and counsellors alike speak of the rapid rise of what they call 'consumptive disorders'. Symptoms include chronic boredom, alienation and the inability to concentrate for more than short periods at a time, as well as a sense of meaninglessness, low self-esteem and an increase in violent behaviour. These are the result, at least in part, of life lived in a hyper-materialistic society at a sustained level of constant overstimulation. The diagnosis of depression has increased tenfold in western countries in the last 30 years. Sales of anti-depressants have hugely increased. Annual sales of Prozac in Britain are higher than the GNP of many developing countries. Stress is now one of the top five causes of health breakdown.

Small world

There has been a growing awareness of the sheer injustice of this way of life. The western consumer lifestyle, even when responsibly exercised, is resourced by a system of massive and sustained inequality.

A presentation at the Eden Project in Cornwall asks us to imagine the world's 6 billion people shrunk into a village of 100 people. With existing ratios remaining the same there would be 57 Asians, 21 Europeans, 14 from the western hemisphere, and 8 Africans. Of these, 80 would live in substandard housing, 70 would be unable to read and 50 would suffer from malnutrition.

We usually ask the wrong question at this point. The puzzle is not why God allows the poor to starve. The scandal is why God allows the rich not to share.

In search of a Christian response

The issues that shape the way we live are extremely complex and the pressures they bring with them are huge. Perhaps it is not surprising to find the Christian Church struggling to express clear, practical alternative ways of living. Consideration of the environment, the economy and social ethics are now higher on the agenda of most Christian agencies than they have ever been, yet it is hard to sustain the discussion at a popular level. Never was a debate more needed. A Christian understanding of choice in a society with a radically inflated and disordered desire is an important part of that task.

Three affirmations form the basis of this discussion:

Our human vocation is to be choice-makers

This is God's gift and intention for humanity. The creation stories reveal our calling to know ourselves through the responsible exercise of choice. Christian responsibility is found in celebration, gratitude and the same joyful self-abandonment that reflects the character of the Creator.

All the evidence is that our society finds exercising responsible choice extremely difficult. We are a culture characterised by compulsive and addictive behaviour patterns. Life is reactive rather than proactive. The reason that so many seek counselling lies in a sense of personal powerlessness, of having no choice. A key strategy in helping people through stress is to enable them to understand and to manage their own personal choices. Responsible and creative choice-making has become a lost vocation of our times.

A Christian response needs to be sensitive to this. I once heard a preacher castigating this selfish society where people 'choose to do what they like when they feel like it'. He compared this to being Christian. Pausing dramatically, he said, 'Frankly, we have no choice!' He spoke with great authority. We all nodded in agreement. This was *real* commitment to Jesus. The message I heard at the time, I confess with some relief, was that we could leave the more difficult issues to God. But he was wrong. Christian discipleship is a call not to choiceless obedience but to responsible freedom. The Bible is full of challenges and invitations to make choices and decisions.

Jesus lived in unbroken commitment to his Father's will, but his life was full of personal choices and decisions. The reality and cost of this is seen most vividly as he anticipates his own suffering and death. Right to the end he is making choices. In the Garden of Gethsemane he sweats blood over the decision he faces (Luke 22.44). On the cross he tastes the bitter wine he is offered to dull his pain, but chooses not to drink it (Matthew 27.48). With his final breath he chooses to surrender his spirit to the Father (Luke 23.46).

The beginning of Christian faith is the restoring of our vocation to be choice-makers. There is a right, creative and health-giving exercise of will at the heart of Christian discipleship.

To be able to affirm 'I want to . . .', 'I intend to . . .', 'I desire to . . .', 'I decide to . . .', is a right and important exercise of will. Of course we will not necessarily make right choices, or wise choices – they may not yet be Christian choices. But the beginning of responsible and faithful living is found here.

Our choices express our belonging

We have seen how closely the consumer lifestyle is linked to our search for personal identity. But the ultimate question at the heart of choosing is not what we wish to acquire, but what kind of world we are seeking to be a part of.

Consumer talk about 'freedom of choice' is meaningless unless we ask what kind of freedom is being talked about. The freedom to buy my favourite trainers or jeans looks very different when I am told the wages and working conditions in a factory in the Far East that my choice demands.

Social institutions that once stood outside the market place are now for sale like everything else. Education is one example. The idea of 'parental choice' drives education policy. Schools now compete as education providers. But in reality 'parental choice' is a freedom only for those who can afford it.[3]

Part of the crisis of education is that we have lost a consensus as to what it is for. The context of learning cannot be separated from what is learned. The process is part of the content. What place have the words 'private' and 'independent' in a process that prepares the growing generation for responsible participation in the struggles, longings and hopes of a whole society?

It is here that the Bible's teaching on wealth and possessions offers an important insight. The Bible itself is not as hostile to wealth as is commonly supposed. But it does warn that wealth brings powerful temptations and distractions. To be wealthy is not a sign of particular favour or status. It brings with it important responsibilities.

But there is a certain kind of wealth and lifestyle that is furiously attacked wherever it emerges in the world. The Hebrew word *betsa* usually means 'desire' or 'longing'. There is nothing wrong with those things. But this is a particular kind of longing. The word is also variously translated as 'covetousness' or 'ruthless greed' or 'dishonest gain' (Jeremiah 22.17). It is a fierce, blunt word that carries a passionate social vision behind it. *Betsa* is a lifestyle based on unbridled ambition, pursuit of power and personal gain lived in total disregard for the community as a whole. Just as it does today, *betsa* can have the outward appearance of moral respectability and even deep religious devotion.

In the New Testament the word that captures the same concern is *pleonexia* – 'greed', 'avarice'. It is often bracketed with promiscuity and adultery (Mark 7.21 and Colossians 3.5).

The horror of *betsa* lies in its utter disregard for the good of the whole. The evil of *betsa* is that it conspires to destabilise the ordering of the whole. The antidote to this is found in the word *epiekes*. Here the translations help us even less. It is usually translated 'moderation' or 'gentleness', which suggests little more than well-intended but ineffectual niceness to all. The word means something very different: 'It means matching, a toning in with the whole, an awareness of how one's own small piece fits into the jigsaw picture. The word is concerned with knowing how a person fits into the life of the whole.'[4]

This kind of living recognises the delicate balance of interdependence and responsibility. It is far more than sharing goods with those less fortunate than us. It is not even primarily about actions. It is concerned with belonging and relationships. This is the vision of a world in which all things hold together.

The growing awareness of just how vulnerably interdependent life actually is has been one of the reforming insights of modern science. We have yet to apply the same truth to human society.

Christian choosing is made in the midst of suffering and resistance

Christian choosing can be expressed in the willingness to remain hungry rather than be filled. Jesus speaks a special blessing on those who hunger and thirst for righteousness in this world: 'They will be filled' (Matthew 5.6). Christian choosing involves cross-bearing. It means being willing to live from a divine discontent at the way life is. To live in penitence at our complicity with systems of discrimination. To live in costly identification with the suffering victims of an unfair world. We point to a kingdom that is coming and seek to live lives that reveal its breaking-in. The Christian communion finds its truest meaning in this context. Some churches have a practice of carrying bread and wine up to the altar to be consecrated, broken and shared. Words of offering are spoken. In one form of these God's people are challenged as to what they are doing:

What do you bring to Christ's table?
We bring bread,
Made by many people's work,
From an unjust world
Where some have plenty
And most go hungry.

At this table all are fed,
And no one is turned away.
Thanks be to God.

What do you bring to Christ's table?
We bring wine,
Made by many people's work,
From an unjust world
Where some have leisure
And most struggle to survive.

At this table all share the cup
Of pain and celebration,
And no-one is denied.
Thanks be to God.

These gifts shall be for us
The body and blood of Christ.
Our witness against hunger,
Our cry against injustice,
And our hope for a world
Where God is fully known
And every child is fed.
Thanks be to God.[5]

CHAPTER 9

Hide and seek
Ambivalence, concealment and flight from desire

> People often feel most alive while they are escaping.

ON LONG family walks our strategy for reviving flagging energies is to play hide-and-seek. We take it in turns to run ahead while the rest cover their eyes and count to 30. Then we go searching for each other. It never fails.

Hide-and-seek must be the oldest game in the world. But what is it about? Its enduring popularity and the unfailing buzz it brings suggests something very important is being acted out, and we instinctively know it.

This game of hiding, losing, searching and being found is actually very ambivalent. What we really want is never quite clear. The thrill of escape, the need to find a 'safe' hiding place, to be unseen, against the 'threat' of someone's imminent search ('Coming, ready or not!'), is always exhilarating. But the game would not work without the knowledge that someone will come searching for us.

In hide-and-seek to lose is to be found. But hiders will often be their own betrayers. If the escape has been too effective, if there is a risk that we won't be found, we will cough, shout clues or jump out and reveal ourselves. We must not escape too efficiently. For children or adults, hide-and-seek acts out a mixture of conflicting desires.

The vocation to desire

What feelings or associations come to mind when you hear the word 'desire'? We must avoid the easy temptation of lumping our desires into the general basket of passions and senses – the random collection of impersonal instincts and blind impulses that offer stimulation and excitement in our private worlds (or threaten to overrun and possess them). Desires are not a question of what we are feeling. Desire is more than passing moods and whims. Although feelings may be involved, desire is much deeper than feeling or even passion. Our desires are an expression of the deepest truth about ourselves. Discerning our desires will actually draw us closer to the mystery of who we are and our place within all that makes up our world.

But our experience of living leaves us with such basic uncertainties and confusion about who we are that a great deal of careful hiding, concealing and avoiding is felt to be necessary for our welfare and safety. Simply because our desires flow out of the deepest mysteries of who we are and what we truly seek, that may be reason enough for choosing not to know.

Ways of escape

In *Houdini's Box*, psychotherapist Adam Phillips suggests a great deal of modern living is shaped around a fundamental need to avoid meeting our desires. Phillips is not saying our society avoids feelings and desires as such. Far from it. He is suggesting that we act out a complex game of hide-and-seek in which we use our desires to avoid facing our desires. We are a culture 'in flight from confusion and uncertainty about our desires and what we really want'. So vital is this task of escape 'that we must even hide from ourselves the fact we are escaping. It is as though, if we can keep ourselves sufficiently busy escaping, we can forget that that is what we are doing.'[1]

It may seem an unlikely hypothesis at first glance. If we deeply want something why should we go out of our way, consciously or unconsciously, to avoid it and seek something else instead? But in our more honest (or despairing) moments, we will admit that our desires and wants are rarely straightforward. They are not what they seem. They can mislead us hopelessly. 'I was so sure that was what I wanted, but . . .'

So we want to hide from our desires because they disturb and discomfort us. What is the discomfort in desires? They unsettle us and make us restless. Our desires remind us we are incomplete.

So they constantly disable us in our attempts at self-sufficiency. They undermine all our projects aimed at establishing secure defences around ourselves. They force us to face change and to make choices. The simplest needs expose us. Nor do our wants and desires come to us unified, organised and prioritised. They are many and often contradictory. They can feel chaotic. We can find ourselves at the mercy of a host of conflicting hopes and longings.

To be open to our desires is to be vulnerable to what we need but cannot control. It requires a willingness to hunger, to yearn, to grieve, to dream.

It takes time to open up, to trust and hope and to risk desire in a world like ours. It may be because life has actually hurt us. It may simply be that we have learned to fear being hurt. We have learned to protect and conceal for so long that our defences are strong and powerful against the invitation to open the door. We have been playing hide-and-seek for so long we have forgotten that it is still, in fact, a game and that there are other ways of living.

We don't lightly choose to deny our desires and live somewhere else. We may even have good reasons for doing so. Our escape attempts take different forms.

The safety of not expecting

One way of avoiding the vulnerable demands of desire is to doubt that in this world they are possible at all. This may be an aggressively cynical attitude to what life offers, or just a quiet withdrawal and disengagement. Either way offers a place of relative safety that avoids the pain of disappointment.

The central character in Niall William's novel, *As It Is in Heaven*, had long lived like this. Stephen is a cautious, vaguely lost young man, older than his years. On the surface he appears to live without any passion or wants at all. He is described as 'too long accustomed to the ordinariness of his own unremarkable history to suppose his life could catch fire'.[2] His life has never been very exciting or desirable so it probably never will be; but that is not his real reason.

As the story unfolds this is revealed as a carefully laid defence. He has never recovered from the tragedy of losing his mother and sister in an accident some years before. It becomes clear that his unexcitable persona is an attempted escape from exposure to hope, longing and wanting anything. Suddenly, out of the blue, he falls helplessly in love. Desire, long kept locked in his depths, is powerfully and irresistibly awakened. He wants to flee and draw near at the same time. He is mortally afraid and joyfully exhilarated by turns.

He struggles with the powerful urge to convince himself that this cannot be real and possible. He is 'too certain that the moment the walls around him were breached he would not be able to bear the incipient grief and loss he associated with love'.[3] And there we come to the heart of his pain. His defence against desire is actually a terror of loss and death.

The refuge of the unattainable

This escape takes the form of always being attracted to things that are just out of reach, things that are never quite possible. Commenting on the recurrent personal struggles of a mutual acquaintance, a friend suggested, 'She needs to face her desire for the unattainable.' It is important to get this just right. If the object of our desire is pitched too high then we will be exposed as unrealistic and challenged to revise our hopes. The game is this: Whatever it is you choose to desire, make sure you are not likely to achieve it. You can avoid having to live with what you want. If you desire the unattainable, you can desire without fear of contradiction. It will be a noble failure. You will be surrounded with much sympathy.

The fault always lies with the people, circumstances, organisations that surround you – and even God. Nowhere and no one will ever fulfil your desires (though of course you were not asking for much!). It could be your church, your marriage, family or work. Once your desires are safely out of reach you will never have to bear the responsibility of living with them – of having them tested in the crucible of committed relationships.

Keeping waiting out of wanting

Another way to avoid actually having to relate to the complexity of our desires is simply to give in to them promptly and without questioning them. (Of course we do not admit this is what we are doing.) This is consumer desire. Our culture is structured to nurture this kind of lifestyle. A thriving free-market economy is dependent on people being stimulated to want and to acquire, but to lose interest quickly in order to rejoin the restless search for new objects of desire. This works by narrowing down our desires to neatly manageable proportions. We cut through the complexity and uncertainty of true desiring. With the uncomplicated directness and confidence of the advertising campaigns we convince ourselves we know *exactly* what we want: 'All I want is . . .' In practice this desiring is characterised by spasmodic and impulsive wanting that quickly becomes restless with what is acquired. The price is high. But we live in a fantasy that we have somehow brought the whole vulnerable and unsettling process of desire under some sort of control.

The parable of the prodigal desires

One of the best-known stories that Jesus told provides an interesting study of desire. It is commonly known as the Parable of the Prodigal Son (Luke 15.11–31). But it is in fact a story about two sons and their father who handle their desires in radically different ways. We should always be suspicious when a story is so evidently misnamed and only told in part.

The younger son is restless. He is full of impatience and goes to his father and demands his share of the family inheritance. Notice he is actually asking for what is rightly his and his desire is not wrong. It may even be a healthy sign that this young adult is ready for more responsibility. But he is asking too soon. For a son to make such a request in the culture of Jesus' day was to insult the father – effectively to wish him dead. What his father feels about this we are not told. But the father gives the son his share – and his freedom.

The son goes to a 'far country'. Did he have to go so far away? Perhaps a symptom of disordered desire is that it always feels like escape. He enjoys himself enormously. No need to be grudging: this is a first taste of freedom. Despite what many people assume, the storyteller does not suggest decadence. It sounds great! But desires and passions do not pay the bills. Money runs out and he finds himself bankrupt. His personal crisis is matched by a crisis in the world around him. There is famine in the land, and he is forced to take work where he can. He, a Jew, ends up tending pigs, and he is hungry enough to eat their food. His life can sink no lower.

But now, in his despair, comes a moment of grace. (Perhaps

not for the first time, but he is now desperate enough to hear.)
Something clicks. The storyteller says 'he came to himself'. This
is a revealing phrase. The 'far country' is not just a physical
place. In some very significant way this young man has been in
exile from himself. He has lived far from his own deepest desires.
He now sees where to his cost 'the compass of his own excitement' has led him, and recognises where he really belongs. He
decides to return home and ask for a place on the most menial
terms. He has surely disinherited himself – 'make me your hired
servant'. He rehearses this speech each step of the long journey
home.

But now the story is interrupted by the unexpected behaviour
of the father. Despite his son's appalling rejection and humiliation
of his name, he has apparently never stopped loving, longing and
watching for him. The moment he sees that forlorn figure on the
horizon he abandons all dignity, gathers up his skirts and runs
down the road to him. The son never gets the rehearsed speech
out. What he had barely hoped to earn, he now receives as an
overwhelming, extravagant gift. Beyond all hope and deserving,
his life begins again in the celebration of the father's desire.

Near and far

The older son is a quite different character. He appears to have
been a model son and heir – reliable, dutiful, responsible and
contented. When his lost brother returns home he is outside,
working. It is quite implausible that he was unaware of the
commotion in the house and of what had caused it. But he stays
outside. So he too is outside the father's house. And the father
comes out to meet him too. His father speaks of his love and
excitement that the son he thought he had lost was home alive.
Now the older son's restraint gives way. Beneath the surface of a
dutiful, loving son a deep well of festering bitterness is uncovered.
He insults his father, accusing him of favouring his brother and
of neglecting him. He disowns his brother – 'this son of yours' –
and castigates his brother's profligate living in terms that suggest
a vivid imagination and probably envy!

This son too is in a far country – a bitter and sterile place full
of self-pity, resentment and anger. He too has squandered the
riches of his inheritance – by taking them for granted and for-
getting to celebrate. He too was a prodigal son. He has never

risked the vocation to enter and know his desires and longings.

Whenever I preach or lead discussion on this story I find that the older son receives overwhelming sympathy. It is not fair: 'You never gave me what I desired.'

The father's reply is very revealing: 'It was all yours to enjoy all along. You never asked.' The older son's inheritance too was there to be entered and enjoyed. But he had left it unused and uncelebrated. He too had lost the gift and privilege of being a son in the father's house. He never renounced it like his younger brother. But there in the field he complains of how he has been a slave 'all these years'. The older son turns out to be a personality eaten away within by unlived, unrisked desire.

In the end, who is furthest from the father's home and love? If the younger son needed to return to his true home from the far country of his own indulgence and impulsiveness, the older son must find a way home from the sterile wasteland of his own 'goodness'.

The first shock of the story – especially to the devoutly religious in the audience – is that the son who risked living most fully and even irresponsibly with his desires actually achieves his true desire. His elder brother – who had never left the father's home, who had never risked any engagement with his passions, never celebrated the free gift of his inheritance – ends in bitter exile.

The prodigal father

What is most often missed in the telling of the story is the third prodigal desire. The most extravagant and wasteful behaviour in this story is surely the father's. No parenting manual would encourage that kind of indulgence in the face of such irresponsible behaviour. But this, says Jesus, is how God loves. The heart of the story is the wildly prodigal desire with which the father loves both sons.

This is, perhaps, the most wonderful and disturbing desire of all. More important than our own desires is the knowledge that we are desired. The deepest awakening of all is to the discovery that we are loved with a wild, prodigal love – without condition. We love, because he first loved us. We desire because God desires us first.

And this will be our greatest struggle. What has prepared us for the terror of being loved without condition and the disabling grace of being undeservingly loved? Like Adam and Eve in the garden, we play hide-and-seek. But God plays too.

Interlude:
On the sound of God sneezing

I am sitting in a remote cabin where I have gone for a week of prayer and writing.

A squirrel has befriended me in my hermitage. Several times a day she lands with a thump on the windowsill, taps boldly on the window and watches me with bright anticipation. Ask and it shall be given to you. I go to get some scraps of food but my slightest move scares her and she vanishes into the woods for several hours. Sometimes I catch sight of her crouching on a tree branch watching me from a safe distance.

We now have a routine. Each time she comes, she finds a trail of apple or bread on the windowsill. It leads her, piece by piece, away from her safety behind the sealed glass to the open window where I wait to meet her.

She works her way along the trail. Behind the glass she is eager, even confident. But as the open window gets nearer she grows more tense — appetite and curiosity battling with fear. The last few pieces by the open window, face to face, take all her courage; several false starts, snatched almost on the run, like a sneak thief.

There is a desire here — an attraction and seeking out that is more than food (though food is where trust is grown for all of us). But that trembling hope, the drawing near that each time risks coming a little closer — I feel it too. For so am I in my desiring. I too watch and long at safe distances and find the boldness to demand from behind safe barriers (though closer than I know). But as the open window nears — face to face, fearful, trembling, this is all I dare; my escape is well planned against your slightest move.

Quick, go! A flight that always feels like wild relief – a perverse liberation. Until the next time, the yearning being strong.
The squirrel has just returned. The ritual begins again. I don't know her desires; nor, perhaps, does she. But we begin again to seek each other.

Then suddenly I sneeze.

She's gone. (How does God's sneeze sound to us?)

CHAPTER 10

The compass of our excitement
Wanting, feeling, waiting, listening

Knowing
what you
want stops
you from
finding
out what
you want.

I WAS SITTING alone in a crowded shopping mall. Nearby towered a brutish vending machine, complete with celestial chimes, rotating lights and a steely synthesized voice. A miserable young lad approached, dragging after him his package-laden mother. He searched her eyes repeatedly until she finally fed the machine, got a Rocket Ranger toy and stuck it out to her child. He slapped it onto the floor and screeched for still another selection. Mum stuffed in more bills until finally the boy was out of choices. 'Well for God's sake what do you want?' she bellowed. In a confused rage the boy bawled, over and over again, 'I want *something*, I want *something*, I want *something*!'[1]

Feeling passionate

What did that child really want? What is he crying for out of that 'ravenous boredom'? How is he to find out? At first glance the question should not be so hard to answer.

Contemporary culture prizes itself on being in touch with feelings. It has been described as a 'culture of intimacy'. The most desired quality to be found in a person these days is 'passion'. OK – but what do you mean by 'passion'? We use the word in very different ways. A random search through a Sunday newspaper found the word in a wide variety of contexts. Articles on politics singled out the lack of 'passion' as a primary concern. 'Prime Minister must inject passion to combat voter apathy,' said one. 'People are contemptuous of passionless double-talk,' said another.

Below that was an advertisement for chocolate – 'dark and passionate'.

On another page, high-street coffee bars were being roundly criticised for their high prices and their low ability to make a decent cup of cappuccino. Not so, replies the spokesperson: 'We at Costa are passionate about serving coffee to the highest standard.'

From inner-city London, there was the encouraging story of a man who had built up a thriving cricket club for boys who were otherwise hanging around the streets. His 'passion for cricket' was giving boys a new interest in life.

My favourite was on the front page. A stunt flying club was offering couples the chance to get married in mid-air – strapped to the wings of a biplane. 'We're really passionate about this,' read the press release.

Passion is about feeling strongly. What we are passionate about is not particularly relevant. It could be chocolate or it might be world poverty. This is what it means to be alive. We follow the 'compass of our excitement'. Wanting and feeling are kept stimulated at fever pitch. But we struggle to discern from those feelings what we are really looking for. What we want is not necessarily what we need. Passionate feeling is not the same as depth of longing. What we want, or long for, may not be what we most deeply desire. Confused? You are not alone. It is all too easy to react to a feeling the same way that we respond to a headache or indigestion. We *take* something for it.

But the painful paradox is that this culture of intimacy is increasingly unable to sustain true intimacy – or any kind of committed relationship. Feelings are no foundation on which to build life. Life has become a constant restless search for sensation, new stimulation. Society is increasingly characterised by addictive and compulsive behaviour of all kinds – shopping, sex, drugs, food, alcohol.

Asking the question

What do you want? Let's start with that question. Finding the answer involves learning to listen to the extraordinary repertoire of fluctuating wishes and longings that offer clues to the mystery of who we are and what we truly desire. But this is not easy.

I was once listening to a man who had come to talk through some areas of his life that he seemed unable to resolve. They were not major problems but he lived with a continual nagging sense of frustration and felt powerless to change the way things were. We talked around the issues and feelings for a while and then I asked him, 'If you could choose, what do you really want for yourself?'

He went silent and then began talking as if in answer, but actually changing the subject. In my experience, people can very rarely answer the question directly and often end up trying to avoid it – though they are usually unaware of doing so. As we talked it became apparent that this man had been taught that to have personal desires or personal wants is selfish. He had given his life to Jesus. 'The cross is "I" crossed out.' He should only want what God wants. His social and family background similarly inhibited of listening to feelings or managing emotions.

For other people the question may expose a deep sense of personal inadequacy and lack of personal confidence. 'I am small and insignificant. No one will be interested in my desires and wants, they are so petty and unimportant.'

Others have never felt any such inhibitions about pursuing what they want. 'I just feel like it' is justification enough. But their lives are filled up with the accumulated jumble of their emotional and material choices. They are quite unable to distinguish a feeling that is a mere emotional reflex and something that comes from the depths. They live under a tyranny of distraction. Clearing a space from which to begin to sort through to real priorities and authentic longings needs considerable time and energy.

Some mixture of these responses is often present when we are invited to give voice to our real wants and desires. But even when we try to answer the question we will often stumble and stammer with the effort of expressing what we want. It is as though we lack the language with which to name and talk about our deeper places.

Facts and feelings

Within church life, worship has been marked by growing informality and warmth of feeling. Intimacy with God is spoken of as the goal of worship. We have come a long way from the formal worship of my childhood: then there was an unspoken understanding that on arrival for worship emotions were to be left in the porch along with the umbrellas. Out of this the discovery of a spontaneous charismatic fellowship felt very liberating. But it was now all feelings. We left our brains in the porch instead! In a Baptist fellowship I first experienced the possibility of thoughtful believing and freely expressive worship in the presence of God. But even then there was a caveat – a catchphrase that was repeated most weeks: 'Remember, we go by facts, not feelings.'

I understood what was intended by this. Feelings are, by themselves, a poor foundation on which to base Christian commitment. But once again the message was that emotions and feelings need warning against. As well as a concern that Christian faith could ever be described, by implication, as objective fact, there was no positive teaching offered about the place of emotions in our life. These hugely energising, shaping, motivating and ever-present passions were left without guidance. They were best not relied on for any contribution to the things that really mattered.

Thinking and feeling are assumed to be opposites. We separate them as mind and heart. This assumption has ancient roots in western philosophy and theology. Influenced by Greek thought, some of the early church teachers (though by no means all) believed that feelings and emotions were part of the inferior, sensual, physical world. Mind and spirit were regarded as superior, and the goal of Christian life was to achieve a passionless state of pure spirit, untainted by earthly passions.

This belief finds no place in the Bible. It is also contradicted by the modern understanding of human consciousness. Our capacity both to think and feel originates in the brain. Tests reveal that human beings respond emotionally when they are thinking and are thinking when they are stimulated by their sensual feelings. The whole relationship is much more subtle and complementary.

Befriending our feelings

Where do we start to build a creative relationship with our feelings?

1 At their most positive, our feelings and emotions are life-

giving, energising. But on their own they are hopelessly mis-
leading. We may feel something with passionate intensity but
still be unclear about what we actually want. The very intensity of our feelings can get in the way of understanding what
they are actually telling us.

2 Feelings can be completely illusory – emotional spasms that
vanish as fast as they come.

3 Strength of feeling is never an excuse for not taking responsibility for our actions and beliefs. Some forms of guidance are
prone to this. 'It felt right', or 'I just know' may well be a
starting-place but will need careful checking out with other
sources of information. Even a couple head over heels in love
and swept along on a torrent of feelings will still need to find
a time for contemplating the gift they share and for discerning
the kind of commitment it may be calling them to.

4 Feelings may be artificial. We may be attracted to something but with ulterior motives. We may want something
badly because it will impress or give us status among our
friends. We may long for something because we fear we will
not be acceptable or liked. As Mark Twain once said, 'We buy
things we do not want, to impress people we do not like.'

5 We must listen carefully and gently to our feelings and moods.
Our feelings are landmarks of a kind, of the personal geogra-
phy of our life story. Our emotional responses to life will have
been shaped by experiences of joy and pain. Feelings are vulnerable. They are easily hurt and wounded. They may carry
scars of misadventure, of life miscarried or betrayed.

Calling by name

In the second story of the creation of Adam, after he has been
given a beautiful garden to live in full of everything good, there
comes a surprising moment. God suddenly declares, 'It is not
good for man to be alone' (Genesis 2.18). Well, was anyone suggesting it was? The reader has the feeling of having missed out
on an important conversation between Adam and God. All we
hear is God's conclusion at the end of it.

There in the original goodness of creation, surrounded by all
the fullness of what God has given, Adam is a creature of unfulfilled longing, of frustrated desire. He feels incomplete. Notice
that this is not a hunger that the presence of God can satisfy.

The story is told of a man who found courage to say in a Christian prayer group how lonely he often felt. 'But Jesus is your friend,' said one well-meaning group member. 'Jesus doesn't play golf!' was his reply.

The search is on, and imagining the next scene is very funny. God sets to work creating vast numbers of animals and birds and brings them to Adam to name. It is a task that demands prodigious feats of imagination, yet it requires something much deeper than that. Remember, Adam is seeking and searching for what he desires. He does not seem to know exactly what he wants or needs. And nor, apparently, does God; at least it is not an answer God can give him. For Adam, it must involve searching, meeting and making relationships. All that lies behind the symbolic task of naming an other.

The long cast list of creatures that Adam meets and names, but without finding what his heart is seeking, serves to build up to the explosive moment of recognition – at last – when he sees Eve. But it is surely also significant that in searching for the single object of his desire, he must engage with the whole created world.

The important thing is that Adam acts on his longings – though at this stage he has not even put them into words. He must follow the ache. With God's help, he goes stalking his desires.

Questioning the ache

When life feels good we are not inclined to disturb things by opening up deeper questions. So the times when our longings feel denied or we do not get what we want are important. We will be tempted to find ways of soothing them and avoiding the insecurity they bring. But they need questioning to begin to understand their significance to us, to others or to God. Our aches, hurts and yearnings may be symptoms of deeper, unrecognised desire.

One way I have found helpful is to write an imaginary conversation with a particular pain or frustration that has surfaced in me. I will introduce myself to my frustrations and invite them to introduce themselves to me. I will write of how I feel about their presence in my life and then give them space to tell how they experience me! Sometimes the ache will not easily find words and I will try to mime the mood or feeling. All the time I seek to honour what is within, in love and trust, and to welcome what it may wish to reveal to me. There may be times when it is wise to share this 'conversation' with a friend or pastor.

Waiting

If the first task is questioning and naming, the second involves waiting. Does anything in our society nurture the positive experience of waiting? Quite the opposite. It is a waste of time and money. We are endlessly attracted to things that make life go faster for us. So our lives are marked by restlessness and we learn to fear the spaces in our lives that might deepen the present moment. This is so much a part of our daily living that we are largely unconscious as to how compulsive our patterns have become. It is so easy, so unthinking to turn on the television, pour a drink, pick up a phone, the moment a space opens up for just too long to be comfortable.

One of Adam Phillips's clients was always in a hurry. When he walked along the street his girlfriend complained she could never keep up with him. In a restaurant he chose quickly from the menu and then sat with thinly concealed frustration while others enjoyed pondering what to choose. He was a man who always 'knew what he wanted' and went straight for it.

Phillips tried to help him explore why he avoided ever being in a place of indecision – the place of waiting between things. Was this a man who really knew what he wanted, or was his decisiveness a need to avoid a deeper indecision and an anxiety about desire? 'Between waiting, wanting and doing something about it there was a terror, a delay that seemed unbearable.' Because he always moved so fast from choice to decision his 'desiring was always premature' and actually provided a short-term surface relief from his deeper and more fearful indecision.[2]

Waiting tests our desires. The Bible is full of exhortations to 'wait'. The real and deep desire will endure and even deepen through waiting. Passing enthusiasms will be seen for what they were. This needs patience. The willingness to wait acknowledges that our desires are dependent on other people, on circumstances and on God for their fulfilment. This needs trust. Waiting exposes us to where our appetites have become compulsions or addictions. This needs healing. Waiting helps us to digest and absorb our experiences of life and to stay in the present moment.

Life needs savouring. Finally, waiting confesses that there are some things so precious, compelling and full of promise that no delay will be too long and no lesser substitute will satisfy. This is faith.

Listening

Waiting makes listening possible. Real listening only happens when we offer our whole attention. But listening to something as volatile or uncertain as our desires and passions takes courage. We may also need the wisdom and support of friends to discern what we are hearing and to know how to respond.

A single woman once found herself, quite unexpectedly, attracted to a married man. She was a Christian. For all the confusion of her feelings she had no wish to pursue a relationship with him and would have considered it wrong. But the attraction was very powerful and she felt extremely vulnerable. She found the courage to speak to a trusted friend. She knew she would find love and sympathy. She perhaps expected to discuss ways of avoiding him, of distracting or burying the feelings.

In fact her friend asked her to take the risk of drawing nearer to her desire. 'Listen to your feelings. What is it that attracts you to this man? You know this relationship is not possible but what are you recognising in his character, faith and approach to living that you know is important to you? You may be discerning the most important qualities you would seek in the man you marry.'

This brave advice led the woman to review the shape of her desires in previous relationships. This led to a new confidence in what she was actually seeking in human love and the commitment of marriage if such became a real choice in the future.

Journeying into desire

So what are our emotions and passions meant to be in our lives? Just that – emotional and passionate. There is something entirely right, Christian and (ultimately) holy about the longing to live richly and freely out of our God-given passions.

But feeling itself is not our goal. Our wantings and longings give us somewhere to start from. They make a beginning possible. With their energy and life, we must go searching.

CHAPTER 11

Working the dark marble
Passion, eros *and the transforming of desire*

> Our
> sexuality is
> the
> playground
> of prayer.

LIKE MANY restless westerners before him, Charles was drawn to the East. He travelled widely until his wanderings finally brought him to a remote region high up in the mountains on the borders of India, Tibet and China. There he came across a Buddhist Lama who changed his life.

He fell completely under the charms of this wise old man. He was spellbound by his teachings, intoxicated by the 'otherness' of the ancient culture and spirituality. He believed he had found the spiritual home he had lacked, whose absence had been the root of his restlessness. He sat at the feet of the Lama and drank it all in with dazzled and uncritical adulation. But after some months he came to a point where he could no longer sustain this emotional and spiritual intensity. He swung from uncritical worship to thinking that he might have been completely deceived. He could only cope with this insecurity by projecting it onto the Lama. Suddenly it seemed obvious: this was all a sham. He had been betrayed. This guru was a complete fraud. He went to the Lama and denounced him in a furious and lengthy tirade. The Lama listened carefully throughout and when he had finished he asked simply, 'Is that all?'

Charles felt even more insulted.

'Is that all?' I have been telling you my deepest feelings, I have been speaking to you out of the heart of my life, and you say, 'is that all?' The Lama smiled and said, 'Charles, being angry is the one honest thing you have done all year. Why are you wasting it? Don't you see it is a gift you must not throw away?

> Think of your anger as a piece of dark marble; you must work it. If you just carry it with you back to Europe, it will make you a hunchback.'[1]

The image of dark marble is hauntingly evocative. It suggests attraction, mystery and threat. The task of journeying into mature emotional freedom – full humanity – involves a dangerous and risky engagement with each other and with ourselves.

In Charles' case the dark marble is his anger. But 'working the dark marble' could express the task of relating creatively and deeply to any of the strong emotions and passions that accompany the gift of being human and fully alive.

The story tells us four basic truths about our relationship to our emotions. First, the importance of personal honesty about what we are feeling – of careful listening to what our emotions are expressing. Second, that our passions are not neutral. They contain enormous power to shape our lives for good or ill. Third, that we have a vocation to learn how to work the dark marble of our passions and emotions – to enter into a creative, maturing relationship with them. Fourth, that this vocation is not an optional extra for those so inclined – those 'into' therapy or 'touchy-feely stuff'. This is the task of being human and being fully alive. This is the narrow way of our humanity.

Befriending our longings

Unless we are able and willing to befriend our desires – however tentatively and fearfully – we will not be able to approach the question of what we want.

This is God's intention. Our human passions and desires are something positively God-given, not a problem to be solved or overcome. Desiring is a natural, 'good' part of being human. Human beings are created to have needs, longings and desires. Some are very trivial; others are profound and shape our life choices. We must seek a relationship with them. They can shape our lives for good – or leave us hopelessly wasted and lost. But to desire is to be human. Nothing is more fundamental. The choice we do not have is to ignore them altogether.

At first, reading the Bible does not seem to offer much positive help. Much of it appears to confirm our experience that emotions and passions are Problem Areas. They need to be firmly denied and defeated. They must certainly not be indulged. In the New Testament there are twice as many negative references to 'desire' as there are positive ones. Surely this teaches us that desires are an experience of human fallen nature; that we must struggle to be rid of them if we are to follow Jesus and grow in holiness.

A word-study on 'desire' in the *Theological Dictionary of the New Testament* agrees: 'Since desire is so bound up with human nature, the Christian needs constantly to be attentive and awake in turning from it. We can conquer it if we constantly allow ourselves to be controlled by the Spirit of God and by the will of God.'[2]

So it is official. Desire is the expression of *sinful* nature. The only relationship we can have is one of endless watchfulness, struggle, rejection. The work of the Holy Spirit is to control us and thus make this possible.

This is not only depressingly pessimistic – it actually distorts what the Bible says on the subject. In fact the Bible could be described as a celebration of desire. But it is also tough and realistic in its teaching. It understands that our desires need to be rightly ordered and directed if they are to become what God intended them to be. They are part of what needs to be converted in us, not rejected and expelled.

The Bible is full of the experience of positive, joyful and 'good' desire. Worship, celebration and the search for God are expressed in terms of passionate feeling and longing:

Whom have I in heaven but you?
And on earth there is nothing I desire more than you
(Psalm 73.25)

O God, you are my God, I seek you, my soul thirsts for you,
my flesh faints for you (Psalm 63.1)

As a deer longs for flowing streams,
So longs my soul for you, O God (Psalm 42.1)

How lovely is your dwelling place, O Lord of Hosts.
My soul has a desire and longing,
to live in the courts of the Lord (Psalm 84.1)

But earthly desiring is also affirmed and celebrated. The Song of Songs is a wild and joyful erotic love poem that expresses the joys and pains of human desiring at its most vulnerable and ecstatic.

The teaching in the Bible against desire needs to be understood in context. The urgency with which the New Testament warns the Christian communities about greed, covetousness and sexual immorality, for example, is a recognition that our desires are easily misdirected and abused. It is *disordered* desire that is the enemy. Among the first Christian converts were many who had been living in cultures every bit as indulgent and profligate with desires as our own. Christian discipleship is nothing less than the tough but joyful reordering, redirecting, and consecrating to the glory of God.

The problem of goodness

Christian teaching offers real and liberating wisdom for the confused world of human passions and emotions. But it is a demanding task and it is not only Christians who are tempted to cope with these wild, confusing and frightening energies by devising various strategies to control, tame or deny their gift. There is plenty of hunchbacked living around.

Part of the trouble is that our vision of goodness is so bland. We need a more vigorous vision of it. I used to play cricket for a local club where I opened the bowling. One Saturday I had a game where everything came together. I bowled fast and aggressively, took wickets. It felt great. As I walked off the field with my team mates the captain came over to me, clapped me on the shoulder and said, 'Well, Dave, you were bowling like a demon today!' There was a brief pause and he suddenly remembered that he was talking to a clergyman.

But what does it say about our notions of goodness that there is no compliment this side of hell that can be paid to good fast bowling? 'You were bowling like a seraph' doesn't have the same bite.

The late Trevor Huddleston, who campaigned against apartheid tirelessly and courageously long before the cause became popular in the West, once startled a group of theological students by declaring, 'I want to impress on you the importance of learning to hate!' To a Christian audience that spent much of its praying repenting of any capacity for anger or a judging spirit, this was shocking. Not many of us see our capacity for anger, let alone hatred, as a quality to be nurtured and encouraged.[3]

Yet the anger and hatred are not problems that need to be got rid of. They are emotions that need to be directed. Direct your anger and hatred against sin and injustice.

This challenges the picture of Christian living as a constant struggle against our weakness; a battle against our capacity for 'falling' into sin. The gospel is much more than a remedy for our weaknesses. It is, more importantly, concerned with the conversion of our strengths. Christian faith is offensive in this world – not defensive. It is the gates of hell that are under threat from the triumph of Good, not the doors of the Church that are under threat from the power of evil.

If we are to be faithful to God's longing for human beings, if we are to be fully and passionately alive, we shall need all the energies God has created within us. We shall not have strength for the task without them. William Blake speaks of the Christian task as 'seeking the form of heaven with the energies of hell'.

This is risky and painful. For those who have been accustomed to living at some distance from their feelings, the deepening encounter with Christ and the life of the Spirit may at first be marked by a disturbing loss of emotional balance. We may be worried about 'losing our tempers'. But some of us have yet to find them in the first place!

The work of the Spirit is to bring us into all truth – and that will include truths about ourselves that we have been effective in avoiding or concealing. But the greater work of the Spirit is to bring us into our full humanity; as Irenaeus said in the second century AD, 'The glory of God is the human person fully alive, and the life of humanity is to see God.' The conversion and redirecting of our emotional energies is part of that gift.

There is an unintended parable of this in a story from the earliest days of the Christian Church. Such was the intensity of spiritual power and life in that community that there was great expectation of healing and blessing. Peter seems to have been a particular focus of attention. His journey into Christian maturity had been painful and turbulent. He was a passionate, clumsy and impetuous man – declaring his love and then denying Jesus. This man became the leader of the new Church. Wherever he was thought to be passing, people carried their sick friends or relatives, 'that even his shadow might heal' (Acts 5.15). We do not normally expect our shadow side to be a healing presence. Our shadow side is the unfaced, or perhaps untamed, side of ourselves and of our personalities that we have good reason for keeping hidden. But this passionate man had not been tamed by the gospel. Here is a glimpse of redeemed and transformed passion in the service of Christ.

The earthiness of desire

Speak of 'desire' and 'passions' today and it will be assumed that you are talking about sexual pleasure. Our relationship to our sexual longings and energies certainly illustrates the sheer complexity, danger and potential of human desiring.

But this has always been an area of ambivalence for the Christian Church. The sheer messy earthiness of human desire has always been an embarrassment. The Church has wrestled with the relationship of 'flesh' to 'spirit' and struggled to believe that it is possible to celebrate human sexuality as a gift of God. As a result it has always been clear in its warnings. Within the Christian community today sexuality remains one of the most divisive and intimidating areas of human living to try to discuss. Sexual longings and desires remain in separate 'earthly' compartments away from what we think praying and loving God involves.

Simply because it is such a powerfully significant and influential feature of our human experience, it cannot be ignored. But there is a more positive reason for paying it attention. Our sexual desires and energies are not only God-given. In the passion and vulnerability of our sexual living we will be expressing, however hesitantly, something of the mystery of God's image and of the glory, power and even vulnerability of divine desire.

In fact Christian teaching on prayer and love for God frequently uses the language of sexual love and erotic desire. During the Middle Ages over 200 commentaries were written on the Song of Songs! But this was always about *transformed* sexual energy. It had been *spiritualised* and thus rendered 'safe'. So celibacy was valued more highly than marriage as the only sure path to the full presence of God.

One consequence of this is that, historically, the great majority of Christian teaching and praying about desire was written by people who had explicitly renounced active sexual relationships as part of their calling to follow Jesus. However, it does not mean they knew nothing of desire – quite the opposite in many cases.

Yet it is one thing for a hermit in the wilderness to say to God 'one thing have I desired', and quite another for someone who has just fallen wildly in love with the man or woman of their dreams, or is who married with three children.

The Church is still struggling to express a vision for Christian desire and vocation that naturally integrates love for God with and through the raw, erotic earthiness of human longing. It struggles to relate Christian love to the multitude of worldly commitments to belonging, loving and creating that *rightly* fill our lives.

When Jesus insists so harshly on leaving or even hating family for the sake of his kingdom (Luke 14.26), he is actually saying that our lives must be founded on right priorities. God has to come first. It is not those things which fill our lives that are wrong, but the very easy tendency to let them rule our hearts and dominate our desires.

Wounded desire

'Our sexuality is where we tumble over our greatest needs and hungers, where the possibility of erotic delight is revealed, the limitations of our self-love are exposed, and pride is purged.'[4] For that reason alone it needs approaching with a care not always apparent in contemporary living. There was an appropriate diffidence about the way that our genitals used to be called our 'privates'. By contrast it has been suggested that we have shifted the fig leaf from our genitals to our face. In so doing we have lost not only the mystery of our sexuality, we have lost the secret of our identity.

Fearfully held at a distance, exploited carelessly for pleasure, or burdened with impossible expectations of fulfilment in relationships, human sexuality is the place where some of the deepest wounding and confusion in our culture is found. Jim Cotter warns that 'when we come to the place of our *wounded* sexuality, healing cannot start from the place of passion'.[5] That will leave us more bruised and hurt than ever.

I remember one man saying to me, 'I've had more women than

you've had hot dinners. But it has taken me too long to realise that it wasn't sex that I wanted. It was friendship. I just wanted someone to hold my hand.' Intimacy is not to be confused with ecstasy. 'Only deep love and gentle touch and steady goodwill can heal'.[6]

Agape and *eros*

There are two Greek words for love in the New Testament – *agape* and *eros*. *Agape* is commonly held up as the ideal 'Christian' love, modelled by Jesus himself and celebrated in the famous meditation on love in 1 Corinthians 13. *Agape* is a universal, all-inclusive, sacrificial, 'spiritual' love. *Eros* represents the more earthy passions and energies that are expressed typically through our erotic sexual desires.

All too frequently, *agape* is taught as the higher, Christian love to be chosen exclusively. *Eros* is the love that must be denied. But the two cannot be separated without harming both. *Eros* is positively needed for our understanding of Christian prayer and formation. *Agape* that avoids *eros* remains a rather bland, lofty ideal. It avoids some of the very places where love becomes specific, particular. *Eros* earths *agape* in real living. It is to *eros* that St Paul turns as an illustration of the love Christ has for the Church when he compares it to the intimacy of sexual union in marriage (Ephesians 5.21–32).

First love

Last thing at night, I have the habit of 'checking on the boys'. Often tired, sometimes burdened by the unfinished tasks of the day, tripping on the clutter of family life, I enter that darkened room – and seem to cross a threshold. The silence is stroked on a rhythmic tide of children's breathing. They are lying in those strange bodily shapes that children call sleep. Their faces, dimly lit by the landing light, are open, receptive – hauntingly vulnerable and trusting. Thomas Merton wrote that in the night all things recover their innocence. It is particularly true of children.

And I am alive and renewed in the first desire – for them, with them, for the home we are creating, the fruit of bodily union and love consummated, the gift of family, the daily mystery of unfolding life. And there is more. This is God's desire. In the formless dark the first word is still spoken, with endless, boundless desire and unquenchable joyful longing. God is with us.

CHAPTER 12

Tears have been my food
Loss, lament and protest

> The substance of grief is not imaginary. It's as real as rope or the absence of air, and like both, it can kill.

'LIFE IS difficult.'

I remember the sense of relief I felt when I first read that sentence. They are the opening words of Scott Peck's book *The Road Less Travelled*. It was as if the line had slipped past official censors somewhere. Something previously unspoken was out in the open at last.

Life is difficult. Not because anything has gone badly wrong. At least not in the first instance. It comes of being born into a world of change that presents us with continual problems and challenges to solve. We are not so much human beings as human becomers. We are creatures in process – growing, changing and developing. Our lives will always be unfinished.

When I quote Peck's words in discussion groups they always provoke a reaction. For some it just sounds too stark and pessimistic. Why not something more hopeful or upbeat – 'life is challenging'? There can be unspoken anxiety about whether Christians should be talking like that at all. Surely being a Christian brings hope and joy? But there are always those who understand exactly what he is saying – it is their experience. They often remain silent. They have learned to keep their struggles private.

Mind the gap

For many, the routine demands of life are struggle enough. Like living with a small but constant loss of blood, life is draining. We do not always find what we want and we simply may not have the energy to go looking. We know ourselves in the gap between a world we hoped for and the world that is present. 'Life is what happens while you are making other plans' (John Lennon). Somewhere inside we know it and grieve. Alongside the pursuit of our desires and dreams, we must build relationships with our frustration, pain and despair.

There can be almost a cruelty about the life in which we feel confined by a host of family, financial or work ties, and about the powerful dreams of unlived life that can well up within us. There may be a host of good reasons why what we long for is unobtainable – at least for the moment because of family commitments, financial constraints, health or lack of opportunity. Why are we given all this life if it can't be lived? All this unused life inside is just going to waste.

There is grief here we must learn to manage – to mourn in the ache of unfulfilled desire. The task is not easy: life is not simple, nor love inevitable. But we have no choice. It is a non-negotiable life task.

Room for grief

'Blessed are those who mourn', said Jesus (Matthew 5.4). This seems a strange and even insensitive saying on first hearing. It is not obvious that those broken by grief are blessed at all. But perhaps the first gift of this teaching is to declare a positive place for negative emotion. There is a blessing for the miserable!

This comes as an immense relief. It means we do not have to pretend. Jesus declares a special place given to mourning in his kingdom. We are to 'weep with those who weep' (Romans 12.15). This means embracing human pain, and seeking to provide a place where it can be honoured and shared. This then dispels the need to *do* anything *with* it. We are not asked to 'make it better'; we must just be there. There is a courteous and compassionate African saying: 'Let in our sister, Grief, who should always have a place by our fire.'

If we can find a place where our pain is honoured and even

blessed then we can stop running from it. In that space other living may now become possible. While we are running away from pain there can be no real joy. Our capacity for rejoicing is in direct proportion to our capacity for sorrow. A great deal of the frantic hyperactivity of contemporary living is simply that we find no safe place to stop. In *The Poisonwood Bible*, Orleanna tells of her way of coping after the death of her child: 'As long as I kept moving, my grief streamed out behind me like a swimmer's long hair. I knew the weight was there but it didn't touch me. Only when I stopped did the slick, dark stuff of it come around my face till I began to drown. So I just didn't stop.'[1]

I was once called to a hospital where a couple had just lost their baby through miscarriage. The nurses were very caring. The tiny foetus was wrapped in a towel and laid on a tray. We gathered round, talked and prayed and wept and committed her to God.

Somehow the word got around. In the months that followed I found myself approached by other women in the parish who needed to talk about their experience of miscarriage or abortion, often many years before. The pain was still fresh. Tears flowed as soon as the story was told. Some had not been allowed to see their baby. No naming or committal had been offered. No matter how long ago it had been, they had all felt required to pick up life again long before they were ready. They had not been allowed to stop with their pain and walk at the pace that grief requires. All this still needed to happen. There was a need for a place of recognition, of a story heard and received by God in the community of his people – of life lost and hearts broken.

Naomi's anger

Squeezed in between the epic, testosterone-driven sagas of Joshua, Judges and Samuel is a very short story about a widow and her daughter-in-law. It is called the book of Ruth.

Naomi had had a tragic life. She and her family had been forced to leave their home because of famine. While they were in a foreign land her husband died, followed by her two sons. In her time there was no group more vulnerable and powerless than widows. She then hears that back home the famine is over and decides to return to Bethlehem. One of her foreign daughters-in-law, Ruth, insists on accompanying her. As Naomi's sad figure appears on the familiar horizon, the villagers in the harvest fields are trying to guess who it is. 'Is it Naomi?' (her name means 'Sweet One'). And now, in her own community of faith, she pours out her pain and anger:

> Don't call me 'Sweet One' – call me 'Bitter One',
> For Shaddai has made me bitter indeed.
> I was full when I went away,
>   But empty Yahweh has brought me back.
> Why call me 'Sweet One',
>   For Yahweh has testified against me,
> And Shaddai has brought calamity upon me
>   And has pronounced evil sentence upon me?
>   (Ruth 1.20–21)[2]

It is rare enough for a woman to be given a voice in the Bible, but this is startlingly blunt language for anyone to use about God. How would a church cope if someone came forward in a service and spoke like that? In the Bible Shaddai is the name for God often used in the context of judging, blessing and cursing. The storyteller casts her complaint in legal form. This is the language of someone who is coming to court to bring a complaint. God is the accused. He has not acted justly. The greatest honour is paid to Naomi at this point. She is not rebuked or patronised. Her theology is not corrected. Nowhere is there any suggestion that she deserved or caused her troubles. She is not quietly taken aside by a member of the pastoral team. No one tries to minister to her or offer bereavement counselling. Her lament is recorded with utmost seriousness. And her business is with God.

Answer me!

A key pastoral task in caring for someone in distress is to help them prepare their personal case against God. First of all this means listening to their story. Quite possibly it has never been heard before. They may never have heard it themselves. The plot will be very confused; details mistaken; incidents may keep being repeated. Raw pain keeps flooding everything. This is neither counselling nor problem-solving. Nor is the listener there as God's defence counsel. God does not need defending. I have a friend who treats this task with such reverence he will speak of searching for someone's 'personal holy scripture'.

The next task is to prepare the list of grievances, making clear in what ways God has let that person down or broken his promises. An indictment must be drawn up. All this must be brought before God.

The willingness to protest, to be angry, to complain against and even rebuke God, is a characteristic of biblical faith. From the greatest leaders, teachers and prophets to a widowed refugee called Naomi – all must raise their voice. If there are times when suffering must be endured there are other times when we must say 'no'. To question and challenge God's absence in times of crisis or because of the apparent injustice of his actions is seen as a legitimate act of faith – not a lack of it.[3]

Over one-third of the psalms – the public worship book of Israel – are songs and prayers of lament. They are full of urgent questioning and impatient petition: 'Answer me when I call, O God!' (Psalm 4.1); 'Why, O Lord, do you stand far off?' (Psalm 10.1); 'Rise up, O Lord, do not forget the oppressed' (Psalm 10.12); 'Attend to me, and answer me; I am troubled in my complaint' (Psalm 55.2).

Lament is closely related to deliverance and praise. Many psalms that begin with shouts of distress end in praise. There is a breakthrough of some kind. The first 18 verses of Psalm 22 describe harrowing distress and suffering. God has apparently abandoned the sufferer. 'My God, why have you forsaken me, why are you so far from helping me?' (22.1). But something happens between verses 21 and 22. It may be a physical rescue. It may be a special gift of grace that makes it all endurable. We are not told.

This is not a journey from doubt to faith. Lament is not the same as doubt. It takes faith to question God and cry out to him like that. It shows how close the person is to God – not how far away. Passive submission requires no faith at all. Lament gives birth to praise and renews it. I am reminded of an African priest speaking of the importance of lament in a nation broken and wasted by years of war and famine. 'Lament is what keeps the Church in the Sudan alive,' he said with fierce conviction. 'We cry out to God and he hears us.'

Learning the language

By contrast the western Church has lost the tradition of lament.

Part of this may be the influence of culture. The British temperament in particular is famous for its stoic reserve and endurance in the face of struggle. Time and again I have stood with mourners after taking a funeral and overheard the bereaved being congratulated for 'being strong'. This means they are not weeping. It says much that we describe tears in terms of mechanical failure. They happen when we break down.

There is no provision for lament in the extensive revision of services of the Church of England. Faithful prayer and living is understood in terms of obedient submission. Lament is largely absent from books on prayer or spiritual life. No articles on 'lament' appear in manuals or dictionaries of pastoral care and theology, though there is extensive writing on suffering and bereavement. But this is not the same. Lament is a very particular theological response to God out of human pain.

The impression given is that Christian faith is somehow above the needs of the cries of protest we read in the psalms. As life is experienced as increasingly chaotic, the strong emphasis of popular Christian worship is on celebrating a God who is firmly in control of events. Recent collections of hymns and songs for public worship contain no resources for lament. The mood is relentlessly upbeat and positive – even in the sections on suffering. This may be bold faithful defiance in the face of temptation to despair. Or it could be a plain denial – a pretence that the world is other than it is and a refusal to embrace the pain.[4]

As the psalms are now seldom read systematically in public worship, we do not have to hear those unsettling cries of anguish and protest within the praise and worship and prayers of God's people. In any case Christian worship has long given itself permission to omit those parts of the psalms we consider too violent or vengeful to be read aloud. The offending verses are put in brackets. But our capacity for violence and evil is not so neatly avoided. It is too dangerous not to be acknowledged.

The tradition of reading psalms that may be far from our own experience reflects a willingness to enter imaginatively into the sufferings of others. 'Remember those in prison as if you were their fellow prisoners, and those who are ill-treated as if you yourselves were suffering' (Hebrews 13.3).

Perhaps the most important thing about the appalling cries for revenge and the death of enemies (of which Psalm 137 is the most shocking) is that the poison of human bitterness is being violently hurled into the one place that can receive it for what it is.

Lament and guilt

Christian forgiveness needs lament for this reason. It may be that we can only really forgive when we have first owned the hatred and pain that surrounds our story. Without that, 'forgiveness' can be a very pious-looking way of avoiding the conflict altogether. Without the tradition of lament, we only have the language of guilt and sin with which to interpret and speak our pain to God. So we confess as sin what should be cried out as protest.

I once met with a man who had asked to make confession. As it was new to him we talked through what we were going to do and how we were going to do it. It became apparent that he was full of pain over certain things that had been happening to him. He felt let down and wronged. He had tried to do God's will but was dismayed by the outcome of his actions. It just wasn't fair. Somewhere inside him was a voice of protest and resentment but no one had ever told him this was a way of praying that the Bible positively encourages. I suggested that we should make another time for confession. First he should find a place where he would not be overheard, and cry out his anger and pain to God. Until he had done that, he would not be ready to confess the place of his own sin within the story. This quite changed the course of his journey.

But I now wish I had not asked him to lament alone. Lament is something God's people own together. It is public. I wish I could have raged and wept with him.

Lament and praise

Lament keeps the praise of God's people honest and down-to-earth. It refuses to allow us to use religion as a spiritual escape from the painful contradictions of the real world. Where there is no place for lament, people will suffer in unresolved silence. Stories will go untold.

I was once in a lively worship service. It was joyful and full of enthusiasm. We came to the intercessions. This was a time when terrible famine was gripping parts of North Africa, and the news bulletins were full of harrowing pictures. We prayed together for the aid agencies, for the starving, for governments to be generous. Our words were thoughtful, sincere but characteristically restrained and polite.

Then from the back came a loud voice with a strong Australian accent: 'Lord, I just don't know what you're playing at. What are you doing?' The honest directness of the prayer cut across the whole service. I was caught between a guilty resentment that our warm joy had been broken into, and relief that a terrible burden of truth had been offered to God. We had not known how – or even whether – we could. The speaker had only recently become a Christian. He had not yet learned how Christians usually pray about such things. I hope he never does.

Lament and belonging

So where do we start? We must learn to sing the Lord's song in a strange land. But we have forgotten the tune and lost the words.

Stories of violence and tragedy cross the world with such frequency that we have come to regard them as the bad weather of our age. I know where to go to find the theological discussion of good and evil and human free will. I have read the political analyses. I know the psychological theories of violence. I join in the prayer meetings and pray for victim and aggressor alike. I sing with longing the great hymns of God's final victory and the vision of a transformed creation. But just now I want to cry out loud for the sheer bloody horror and meaningless chaos of it all.

Lament is the antidote to despair and silence. I want someone to teach me a song to sing over the dying child caught in crossfire, or a prayer for the old man in a freezing refugee camp who weeps as he tries to eat bread made out of grass and dirt. I must learn to cry out with all those who sew in tears the thin thread of their humanity – for numberless millions whose dreams lie crushed beneath useless oppression.[5] I will rage at the power of the rich but the impotence of wealth to change the world. I will call on Shaddai. I want to know how to pray to a God apparently unable or unwilling to restrain evil on the most catastrophic scale.

Out of the desire of the nations and the dreams of
the powerless,

With the anger of the young and the despair of the old,
I will mourn for all desires unknown and for trust
      shattered,
for life miscarried and stillborn hope,
for the means of grace and the hope of glory.

For our sake – and for God's –
we must cry aloud.

CHAPTER 13

The return to the heart
Solitude, conversion and longing for God

> I have one
> desire –
> to
> disappear
> into God.

AN ORDINATION service at a Church of England cathedral – the setting is majestic and the Church is gathered in its most authoritative and assured mood. Nervous ordinands are standing before the bishop to make their public declaration of faith. This is the culmination of an extended and intensive time – the discerning of choice, desire and the will of God. The bishop speaks.

'Do you believe, *so far as you know your own heart*, that God has called you?'

The qualifying clause in that first question always surprises me – the caveat about the heart. Isn't it a cop-out? Shouldn't it all be clear by now? Yet even that moment of solemn faith and commitment must apparently include a confession of agnosticism. An elusive mystery is hinted at. It seems that our understanding of ourselves, our lives and of God all hinge on this – that we know our hearts.

Lift up your hearts

We popularly think of the heart as the centre of our emotions. So it gets caught up in every passing mood, impulse and feeling. Burdened with such diverse expectations it performs as an organ of extraordinary agility, range of expression and baffling unpredictability. Hearts can fly, leap, race, skip or stop altogether. They can be heavy or light, hard as stone or soft as wax, cold as ice or on fire with passion. Depending on your mood you may find yours in your mouth, in your boots or on your sleeve. You can wound, break or melt hearts. They can be won, lost, stolen or given away. You can have a complete change of heart. Hearts can swing between extremes of love and hate, hope and despair for apparently little reason.

Yet for all the restless mobility of this organ we have a puzzling way of reassuring anyone who has acted in a well-intended, but misguided, way – 'At least your heart is in the right place.' And where is that exactly?

In more thoughtful moments we instinctively identify the heart with something altogether deeper and more central to ourselves. When we commit ourselves with 'our whole heart' or long 'with all our heart' we are expressing much more than our feelings. This brings us close to the Christian understanding of the heart. In the Bible the heart is the true centre of a person – the 'real me'. Peter calls this 'the person hidden in your heart' (1 Peter 3.4 RSV). This true self is the source of all that incredible range of expression that makes us human and alive – thought, desire, will, relating. It is the unifying and integrating centre of our whole being.

Deeper still, the heart is found in God. Only God knows our hearts. 'Search me, O God, and know my heart,' prays the psalmist (Psalm 139.23). It is a brave prayer. For if our hearts are a mystery to us it is only partly because of our sin and waywardness – deadly though that is. The more awesome realisation is that we cannot draw near our true selves without entering the eternal mystery of God's own being.

We must learn to pray. But where to start? We are a culture that has profoundly lost heart. The root of our deepest anxiety is found here. 'Lift up your hearts' is the command in the communion service. Well, I would if I could find it!

A place to start

The simplest way to do this is to be still. We need solitude. That means finding somewhere to be alone. Every person of any spiritual depth in the Bible spent significant time alone. Jesus regularly sought time alone and taught his disciples to do the same. 'When you pray go into a room and shut the door' (Matthew 6.6). Just that – no other technique or method. Solitude is its own teacher. The Father waits there in secret.

It seems that people are instinctively aware of the need for this. At a time when attendance at traditional churches continues to decline, the number of people seeking out monasteries and centres of stillness is increasing dramatically.

I regularly take small groups of students to a remote monastery for weekends of silence and contemplation. Few have experienced silence and solitude before, but they are drawn to it. Although almost everything about the setting and lifestyle is strange, I notice how people respond out of some kind of instinctive recognition. They often struggle to put this into words, as if they are awakening to a part of their own selves that they have not met before. But something waits to welcome them. Some speak of a sense of homecoming.

Solitude is something the contemporary Church needs to rediscover for itself. In his classic book *Reaching Out*, Henri Nouwen named solitude as one of the three essential disciplines of the Christian life.[1] By contrast it is conspicuously absent from the most popular presentations about Christian discipleship.

There are perils as well as opportunities in reaching out to the weary hedonism of our age. Vital though it is to be developing strategies for transforming church life, ministry and mission, Christian living can easily become little more than a religious version of the anxious restlessness around us. The pressure to be relevant and get immediate results tempts us to jettison anything that seems out of date or too demanding, or that doesn't immediately communicate and excite. We offer a 'frantic spirituality for a frantic age'. And what do we gain if we fill the whole Church and lose our soul?

Entering

We have found somewhere alone. How does it feel? The stillness may feel a relief. The embrace of solitude is a loving one. God is a friend of silence. But we are not here to escape from anything. Anyone who has tried to spend time in silence will know how quickly mind and imagination fill up with the very people, situations and pressures that consume our living and that we had hoped to leave behind. By withdrawing from the surface of our world we begin to meet it at a deeper level. This is very important to understand. Solitude is the place where we find our true place in the world. Solitude draws us into community, not away from it.[2]

Waiting

Right, what's next? Nothing. We must learn to wait – not just for God but for ourselves. Our innermost self is a secret self. It is elusive and shy. Entering our own depths is rather like going on safari to see wildlife. We crash into the undergrowth, with little awareness of the disturbance we are causing and the threat we pose. There may be tantalising glimpses of the backs of things fleeing in the distance, then nothing. It all seems empty. What we seek stays hidden. We begin to doubt if there is anything there to be found.

While we carry any hope of capturing or using what we seek, it will remain out of sight. The heart is not for taming. We must just sit still and wait. We have to let go of any hope of possessing something as a way of knowing ourselves.

Loss

We tend to stay still as long as it feels good. But as the silence deepens it becomes unsettling. As soon as energy returns we grow restless. Anywhere else and we would be picking up the phone, or turning on the television, going out somewhere – anything to fill the emptiness that is opening up within us. But here the familiar diversions are not available. We learn to leave each other alone. We begin to discover just how much of our activity is an elaborate substitute for living with ourselves, with each other and with God.

There is a monastery chapel I know that has a deep sense of God's presence. I know that as I kneel there I will have to endure the uncomfortable sensation of being spiritually undressed.

A kind of stripping goes on in solitude. The familiar ways by which we recognise ourselves are taken away. We will no longer 'know' ourselves in any way that we can understand. We will feel we are losing our balance. It is certainly confusing. Weren't we drawn into this out of longing to know ourselves and God more deeply? Here we are more in the dark than before. But this familiar self we are losing was part of the cover-up. It is the false self. We created it in wilfulness or because we knew no other way to survive. But here there is nothing to sustain it. It returns to nothing.

Struggle

Christian prayer has been described as 'a preference for the desert'. But those early Christians who withdrew from their world to the solitude of the wilderness were not opting out. Solitude is a turbulent place. It has been described as 'the furnace of transformation'. In the consuming heat it is the impurities that are most apparent at first, as they rise to the surface. We become aware of the polluted, conflicting currents of our own desires and motivations. Here our trusted repertoire of responses is useless. There is no one to impress or manipulate. What we prized as our freedom to choose is now exposed as a helpless bondage of the will to every passing attraction. We are facing the uncomfortable truth of how even what we called 'love' was actually a sophisticated performance, a way of controlling and possessing the object of our desires.

We face our dereliction, our helplessness and need of God. The way is marked by tears and penitence: 'Out of the depths I cry to you, O Lord' (Psalm 130.1). At last we cry from the heart. We have begun to pray.

Encounter

I was kneeling in a dark chapel lit only by the flicker of candles and oil lamps. Around the walls I felt rather than saw the shadowy company of the saints surrounding us as we prayed. Behind me a deep voice with a strong East European accent began to pray: 'Lord Jesus Christ, Son of God, have mercy on me a sinner.' Over and over he repeated it. After a while the prayer was taken up by a voice on the other side of the chapel, and then another. But the words remained the same. I began to be aware of the extraordinary power of this ancient prayer. It wove its seamless thread around and through the centre of my being, into the community and into all the world beyond. It was a prayer without beginning or end. It seemed to rise out of an abyss of human longing and hopefulness. Everything was included in that endless cry for mercy and faith in the name of Jesus.[3]

'Have mercy on me a sinner.' And here, beyond all hope and

deserving, Christ meets us. In the far reaches of our exile from ourselves, from each other and from God, he has searched us out and found us. He waits, humbly, in secret, nearer to us than we are to ourselves, at home in the depths of our infinite need.

Longing

> As a deer longs for flowing streams,
>   so longs my soul for you, O God.
> My soul thirsts for God,
>   for the living God. (Psalm 42.1–2)

Above all else, the heart is a place of longing.[4] The psalmist remembers the deer in the wilderness. It stops often, lifting its quivering nostrils to the parched breeze for the faintest hint of where water may be found. Our human longings are not primarily for recreation. The desert is not a place for luxuries. Water, food and the safe refuge are matters of life and death. We ignore this at our peril.

We are creatures with immortal longings. Our living is marked by a divine restlessness. 'You have made us for yourself,' said St Augustine, 'and our hearts are restless until they find their rest in you.' Anything and everything is caught up in this. In this longing all of life finds its meaning and purpose. This means that all our earthly choosing and desiring are part of something immeasurably greater, more costly and all-embracing.

This longing wounds us. Nothing can heal it. The longing is for God. It leaves us aching and reaching out for more. Not with the dissatisfied restlessness of the consumer. This is the ache of unsatisfied love that has tasted and now longs for an ever-deeper communion. 'The reward of the search is to go on searching. Really to see God is never to have had one's fill of desiring him,' says Gregory of Nyssa. It is a longing that unites us. In the furnace of solitude our desires are not replaced or consumed. They are ignited and directed at last towards their true source. In the fire of divine love, our disordered passions are drawn together from their myriad distractions and forged into a single desire. 'One thing have I desired, that will I seek after, to behold the beauty of the Lord' (Psalm 27.4).

But greater than any longing of ours is the infinite, crucifying yearning with which God seeks us. 'We love because he first loved us' (1 John 4.19). The most hesitant turning of our lives towards him is met with his own generous and overwhelming gratitude. It is all mutual. He comes running to embrace us.

Choice, desire and the will of God.
What more do you want?

Notes

Introduction

Box 'It is no matter of regret to God [that] the universe is not a piece of streamlined engineering. It is meant to be what it is – a free-for-all of self-moving forces, each being itself with all its might, and yet (wonder of wonders!) by their free interaction settling into balanced systems we know, and into the complexities whereby we exist'. Austin Farrer, quoted in John V. Taylor, *The Christlike God* (London, SCM Press, 1992), p. 187.

1   David Ford, *The Shape of Living* (London, Fount, 1997).
2   Part of an imaginary conversation with Jesus in Michael Paul Gallagher, *Dive Deeper – The Human Poetry of Faith* (London, Darton, Longman & Todd, 2001), p. 108, italics mine.
3   The most helpful study of the experience of desire remains Philip Sheldrake, *Befriending our Desires* (London, Darton, Longman & Todd, 2001). This book is indebted to his insights.

1 As it is in heaven

Box 'The incarnation is God's pre-eminent movement towards us, it is his best, most wildly extravagant gesture. Through this daring, reckless invitation we are called to take part in the life of the Trinity.' Sara B. Savage in *Beholding the Glory*, ed. Jeremy Begbie (London, Darton, Longman & Todd, 2000), p. 75.

1   Rubem Alves, *I Believe in the Resurrection of the Body* (Philadelphia, Fortress Press, 1984), p. 7.
2   Savage, *Beholding the Glory*, p. 77.
3   This translation by Gerald F. Hawthorne, *Word Bible Commentary Volume 43: Philippians* (Waco, TX, Word Books, 1983), p. 75.
4   Paul Fiddes, *Participating in God – A Pastoral Doctrine of the Trinity* (London, Darton, Longman & Todd, 2000), p. 72.

2 If God is God

Box A selective quotation from Keith Ward, *God, Faith and the New Millennium* (Oxford, Oneworld Publications, 1999), p. 94.

1   For a fascinating dialogue between scientists and theologians on these themes see John Polkinghorne (ed.), *The Work of Love* (London, SPCK, 2001). A lively debate among evangelical theologians has been triggered by Clark Pinnock, *The Openness of God* (Louisville, Paternoster Press, 1995). He takes the discussion further in *The Most Moved Mover* (Louisville, Paternoster Press, 2001).
2   'The White Tiger', in *R. S. Thomas: Collected Poems 1945–1990* (London, Dent, 1993), p. 378.
3   For a fuller discussion of this see Walter Brueggemann, *Hopeful Imagination – Prophetic Voices in Exile* (London, SCM Press, 1986), chapters 3 and 4.
4   From the hymn 'My God How Wonderful Thou Art' by F. W. Faber (1814–63).

3 'Let there be . . .'

Box 'The play of creation, as we perceive it, has more the appearance of an improvisation than the performance of a predetermined script.' John Polkinghorne, *Faith, Science and Understanding* (London, SPCK, 2001), p. 110.

1   New Jerusalem Bible. I have inclusivised the last phrase.
2   For more background, see Walter Brueggemann, *Genesis* (Louisville, John Knox Press, 1982). This commentary has been an important resource in shaping this chapter.
3   Brueggemann, *Genesis*, p. 28.

4 Where the wild things are

Box Nietzsche, quoted in Pamela Stephenson, *Billy* (London, Harper Collins 2001), on title page.

1   Maurice Sendak, *Where the Wild Things Are* (London, Picture Lions/HarperCollins, 1963).
2   Thornton Wilder, *The Bridge of San Luis Rey* (London, Penguin, 2000).

3   I am grateful to my colleague Dr John Bimson for his insights on the book of Job and for access to his lecture notes on Leviathan and Behemoth.
4   From a prayer card created for the 1998 Lambeth Conference.

5 Undesirable Saviour

Box Attributed to Dr Frank Lake.

1   The full story is told in Frank Lake, *Clinical Theology* (London, Darton, Longman & Todd, 1996), pp. 794–5.
2   The interpretation of the cross in this chapter has been strongly influenced by the writings of René Girard. James Alison, *Knowing Jesus* (London, SPCK, 1993) is a very accessible Christian application of Girard's theories. Rowan Williams' profound meditation on violence, *Writing in the Dust – Reflections on 11 September and its Aftermath* (London, Hodder & Stoughton, 2002), applies and develops Girard's understanding of victimhood and scapegoating.

6 Ashes and kites

Box 'If grace is true, you must bear the true, not imaginary sin. God does not save imaginary sinners. Be a sinner, and sin boldly, but trust and rejoice in Christ even bolder, who is victor over sin.' Martin Luther's words come in a pastoral letter to an anxious friend. Imaginary sinners are those who define sin in terms of wrong doings. They are in grave danger of self-justification. Life preoccupied with avoiding lapses is not Christ-centred and leads us away from the gift of grace. It can also lead to a certain kind of anxious, separatist and safety-first approach to living, fearful of compromise – as if sin is something you can withdraw from in this world. Luther argues that real sin is actually our radically fallen humanity and separation from God. We all share in this. We are helpless to avoid it or resolve it of ourselves. We must confess it and live in it boldly. So Alexander Jensen concludes, 'Luther's "sin boldly" is definitely not a moral "free ticket", encouraging immorality, but a morally most serious matter, leading to freedom and responsibility'. See his 'Martin Luther's "Sin Boldly" Revisited: A Fresh Look at a Controversial Concept in the Light of Modern Pastoral Psychology', *Contact: Interdisciplinary Journal of Pastoral Studies*, no. 137 (2002), p. 2.

1   Michael Mitton, *Wild Beasts and Angels* (London, Darton, Longman & Todd, 2000), pp. 17–23.

2   David Martin, 'Taking a Stand at the Crossroads', *Third Way*, February 2002, p. 19.

7 In the will of a willing God

Box 'Once for all, then, a short precept is given you: love – and do what you wish . . . Let the root of love be within, of this root can nothing spring but what is good.' St Augustine, *Homilies on the Epistles of St John*, 8: 7.

1   See Eugene Petersen, *Five Smooth Stones for Pastoral Work* (Leominster/Grand Rapids, Gracewing/Eerdmans, 1992), pp. 76–8.
2   See, for example, David Hay, *Religious Experience Today* (London, Mowbray, 1990) and David Hay with Rebecca Nye, *The Spirit of the Child* (London, Fount, 1998).
3   This story is quoted in John V. Taylor, *The Christlike God* (London, SCM Press, 1992), p. 38. The implications of these ideas for Christian pastoral care and mission was a lifelong interest of John Taylor. See chapters 1 and 2.
4   Niall Williams, *As It Is in Heaven* (London, Picador, 1999), p. 60.
5   Thomas Merton, *Thoughts in Solitude* (London, Burns & Oates, 1975), p. 81.

8 You did not choose me, I chose you

Box Niall Williams, *As It Is in Heaven* (London, Picador, 1999), p. 81.

1   See for example Paco Underhill, *Why We Buy* (London, Orion Publishing, 2000). The strap line on the cover challenges the reader, 'For you, the modern day consumer, is resistance futile?'
2   This was a favourite theme of Thomas Merton. See *New Seeds of Contemplation* (Wheathampstead, Anthony Clarke, 1961), pp. 34–5.
3   See Rowan Williams, *Lost Icons* (Edinburgh, T&T Clark, 2000), chapter 1 for an extended discussion on the meaning and exercise of choice in contemporary society.
4   See John V. Taylor, *Enough Is Enough* (London, SCM Press, 1975), chapter 3: 'The Theology of Enough', pp. 45–6.
5   Janet Morley (ed.), *Bread of Tomorrow – Praying with the World's Poor* (London, SPCK/Christian Aid, 1992), p. 170, italics mine.

9 Hide and seek

Box Adam Phillips, *Houdini's Box* (London, Faber and Faber, 2001), p. 3.

1   Phillips, *Houdini's Box*, p. 51.

2   Niall Williams, *As It Is in Heaven* (London, Picador, 1999), p. 81.
3   Williams, *As It Is in Heaven*, p. 70.

10 The compass of our excitement

Box Adam Phillips, *Houdini's Box* (London, Faber and Faber, 2001), p. 114.

1   John Shumacher, 'Dead Zone', *New Internationalist*, July 2001, pp. 34–5.
2   Phillips, *Houdini's Box*, pp. 112–18.

11 Working the dark marble

Box Angela Tilby, 'Prayer and Sexuality', in Fraser Watts (ed.), *Perspectives on Prayer* (London, SPCK, 2001), p. 94.

1   Andrew Harvey, *A Journey in Ladakh* (London, Jonathan Cape, 1983), pp. 194–5.
2   Fraser Watts (ed.) *Theological Dictionary of the New Testament* (Exeter, Paternoster Press, 1975), p. 457.
3   This anecdote is supported by the following quote in his biography: 'We have forgotten how to hate. We must hate what is evil. Apartheid is the most evil thing in the world.' R. Denniston, *Trevor Huddleston* (Oxford, Macmillan, 1999), p. 209.
4   Tilby, *Perspectives in Prayer*, p. 94 – this is the completion of the quote at the beginning of the chapter.
5   Jim Cotter, *Prayer at Night* (Sheffield, Cairns Publications, 1991), pp. 63f. This edition includes a final selection of profound prayers and meditations on the themes of sexuality and spirituality.
6   Cotter, *Prayer at Night*, p. 63.

12 Tears have been my food

Box Barbara Kingsolver, *The Poisonwood Bible* (London, Faber and Faber, 1999), p. 433.

1   Kingsolver, *The Poisonwood Bible*, p. 433.
2   This translation from E. F. Campbell, *Anchor Bible Volume 7: Ruth* (New York, Doubleday, 1975), p. 62.
3   For a fuller discussion see Eugene Petersen, *Five Smooth Stones for Pastoral Work* (Leominster/Grand Rapids, Gracewing/Eerdmans, 1992). See 'II: The Pastoral Work of Story-Making',

and 'III: The Pastoral Work of Pain-Sharing'.

4 The songs and liturgies of the Iona community are honourable exceptions to this.

5 'Like you and I, they too sew the thin thread of their humanity'. The image is borrowed from 'Priestly Duties', a poem by Stewart Henderson, in *Limited Edition* (Stratford upon Avon, Plover Books, 1997), p. 18.

13 The return to the heart

Box 'I have only one desire, the desire for solitude, to disappear into God, to be submerged in his peace, to be lost in the secret of his face.' Thomas Merton, *The Sign of Jonas* (London, Sheldon Press, 1976), p. 16.

1 Henri Nouwen, *Reaching Out* (Grand Rapids, Zondervan, 1998). Nouwen summarised the three movements of the spiritual life as 'Loneliness to Solitude', 'Hostility to Hospitality' and 'Illusion to Prayer'.

2 I therefore consider that solitude is a community responsibility. It is too easy to think of solitude as something certain individuals and temperaments are drawn to. Our corporate living needs to learn to honour the spaces between us.

3 There is growing interest in the practice of the Jesus Prayer. Two very accessible introductions are available: Brother Ramon and Simon Barrington-Ward, *Praying the Jesus Prayer Together* (Oxford, Bible Reading Fellowship, 2001); and Simon Barrington-Ward, *The Jesus Prayer* (Oxford, Bible Reading Fellowship, 1996).

4 For a much fuller discussion of the theme of longing, see Margaret Magdalen CSMV, *Furnace of the Heart* (London, Darton, Longman & Todd, 1998).